T0277665

"A rarely examined look at our fair city's recent, raucous past through its cemeteries. Beth Winegarner's book traces the history of San Francisco through its forgotten cemeteries: their beginnings, their relocations and the bodies that often remain. I thought I knew my beloved city, but I wasn't looking deep enough—literally. Unique and eye-opening, I won't be able to walk these San Francisco streets without wondering what may still be buried just underfoot."

—Caroline Paul, author of *New York Times* bestseller
The Gutsy Girl: Escapades for Your Life of Epic Adventure

SAN FRANCISCO'S FORGOTTEN CEMETERIES

A BURIED HISTORY

BETH WINEGARNER

Foreword by Roberto Lovato, author of *Unforgetting*

THE
History
PRESS

Published by The History Press
Charleston, SC
www.historypress.com

First published 2023

Manufactured in the United States

ISBN 9781467154925

Library of Congress Control Number: 2023937158

For the forgotten dead.

A people without the knowledge of their past history,
origin and culture is like a tree without roots.
—Marcus Garvey

CONTENTS

FOREWORD

I grew up believing that my hometown, San Francisco, was the city in the clouds. I believed this not because of the advent of the Silicon-powered amnesia of cloud storage and other digital innovations but because the city lacks the rootedness that's provided by burying its dead nearby. My Salvadoran immigrant ancestors who were buried here all have plots in the place where San Francisco outsourced its dead: the perpetually foggy suburb of Colma. Most native San Franciscans I grew up with also buried their loved ones there.

These facts of life and death in the Bay Area led me to write about what the Greeks called *aletheia*, which referred to the journey the dead took into the underworld. The Greeks believed that before entering either Hades or Elysium, the dead had to cross the Lethe River, or the river of forgetting, where those who died had to forget who they were in life. *Aletheia* (literally "not Lethe") also means "unforgetting," which the Greeks also equated with "truth," "unconcealment" and "revelation"—all words that describe the important work of Beth Winegarner's *San Francisco's Forgotten Cemeteries: A Buried History*.

Beth's mix of journalism, investigative work and storytelling represents a major step toward historical justice. This book is an act of unforgetting, both for those buried in the countless graves in the San Francisco underworld and for the stories still buried there—especially those of immigrant and indigent San Franciscans of the nineteenth century and earlier. Until now, these stories been paved over and left behind.

Unlike Paris, which houses the bones of millions in the catacombs of the City of the Dead below the City of Light, San Francisco preferred to push its dead into the margins of memory and identity. It is no coincidence that the current epic marginalization of the living by Silicon Valley and other powerful interests takes place on the same land where the dead were also gentrified and marginalized.

From this perspective, *San Francisco's Forgotten Cemeteries* is an act of restorative justice.

My own work in documenting the efforts of forensic scientists to find and excavate the bones and bodies buried in Latin America's continent-wide chain of mass graves taught me about a concept known as memoria historica. Memoria historica refers to the deployment of memory in the pursuit of justice. In writing this book, Beth Winegarner provides the people of San Francisco, the amnesiac city in the clouds, an urgently needed path toward redemption.

Roberto Lovato

ACKNOWLEDGEMENTS

This book wouldn't exist without S.J. Farrer, whose online talk about corpse roads in the United Kingdom inspired me to explore which San Francisco streets once led the way to our cemeteries. And I also have much appreciation for Lydia Chávez, the executive editor at *Mission Local*, for publishing the results of that research in October 2021—and for indulging in my obsession with creepy San Francisco history more generally.

I'd like to express my deep gratitude for my editor Laurie Krill for recognizing the appeal of this book and helping me shape it into the volume you're reading now. And thanks to the team at The History Press for taking me on board and for continually expanding readers' understanding of history—especially local history—which is where the good stuff is.

I also couldn't have written this book without the support and insights of several historians, archaeologists and fellow cemetery nerds, including Woody LaBounty, Kari Hervey-Lentz, Alex Ryder, Elizabeth Creely and Courtney Minick. When I talk with you, I feel like I've found my people.

I have a huge amount of appreciation for the researchers who came before me, particularly John Blackett of the San Francisco Cemeteries website, the team at SF Genealogy and everyone at the California Digital Newspaper Collection, where almost all of the newspaper quotes and clippings in this book came from.

Special thanks and love to my writing coven: Stephanie Wildman, Bridget Quinn, Ann Kim, Jenny Qi, Lyzette Wanzer and Saila Kariat, who held space while I wrote this book and listened to me as I figured out how I wanted to tell the story of San Francisco's cemeteries. And to my early readers, Stephanie, Annise Gross and Rachel Chalmers; your feedback improved the book immeasurably.

Getting the story of City Cemetery into *Alta* in October 2022 was a watershed moment for this book; much gratitude goes to editor Blaise Zarega for working with me on the piece and Beth Spotswood for talking with Woody and me about it so the *Alta* audience could learn more. Thanks, too, to my colleague Rita Chang-Eppig for her insights and to Grace Won of radio station KALW for talking with me about the article (and the forgotten girls of San Francisco's Magdalen Asylum) for *State of the Bay*.

So many others rallied around me as I put San Francisco's cemeteries into words, particularly the Weird Siblings and my partner and daughter. You all were the wind at my back. Particular thanks to two fellow Writers Grotto members, Roberto Lovato and Caroline Paul, for bolstering my words with your own. Thank you so much.

Finally, thank you to all the dead of San Francisco; it's an honor to tell your stories.

INTRODUCTION

I t is a sunny, chilly November afternoon when I step out of my car and begin looking for my mom's grave. I don't live nearby, so I'm only able to visit once in a while, and it seems like it's in a different place every time. Full, mature oak trees arch over the graves, and the ground is carpeted with golden-brown oak leaves and chestnut-colored acorns. The grave markers here are on the smaller side—no large statues or family tombs, just rambling rows of stone and wooden monuments, each a few feet tall. My mom was cremated, and her small grave is marked by only a stone flat on the ground, making it more difficult to spot when the leaf litter is thick.

Finally, I find it, the edges covered in leaves fallen from the olive tree overhead. I brush them back from the dark gray gravestone, making sure she isn't hidden away, and I quietly say, "Hi, Mom." Behind me, several wind chimes hang from the branches of the tree, and a soft breeze blows past, ringing them. "Is that you?" I whisper.

Forestview Cemetery, located just outside my hometown of Forestville, California, was founded sometime in the mid- to late 1800s. Fredrick Faudre was just thirteen days old when he became the first person buried on this hillside plot in April 1865—how his parents must have grieved. The next recorded burial was that of George Rickett, who was only five and a half years old when he joined Frederick here in 1877. At least, those are the earliest records we have.[1] Forestville was first occupied in 1834, when John B.R. Cooper established the state's first known power-operated commercial sawmill here, but it didn't become recognized as a town until 1879, by which

The entrance to Forestview Cemetery in Forestville, California. The cemetery was established sometime in the 1860s. *MikeVdP/Wikimedia Commons, licensed under the Creative Commons Attribution-Share Alike 4.0 International license.*

time it was only six blocks of homes, businesses and a saloon owned by Andrew Jackson Forrister.[2] Why it's not called Forristville is anyone's guess.

Since those early days, only a thousand or so people have been buried in this five-acre graveyard, and there's room for more. Often, when I visit, I'm the only one here, even though several more people have been interred here since 1996, when my mom died, and I suspect pretty much all of them were locals, likely with family nearby. Sometimes, when I come here, I wonder why I do it. Often, I feel like my mother is with me physically, if not in spirit; she is literally in my DNA, in my blood and bones, in the goofy jokes I make with my daughter and the deep calm I feel when I'm sewing. And there are times when I think I can hear her voice or feel her hand on my back, supporting me. But if she's with me so viscerally, why do I come to her grave, sweep it off and spend time in the place where we buried her ashes? If our spirits leave our bodies when we die, why do we visit our loved ones in cemeteries, where only the remains of their bodies are located? Do we believe their spirits return to these places when we drop by, and do we expect their graves to remain in one place forever—or at least until they are lost to living memory?

The cemeteries of San Francisco, where I now live, raise every one of these questions and many more. Between the founding of its first settler cemeteries in the 1770s and its ban on burials in the early 1900s, the city was home to roughly thirty large and small burial grounds. There were cemeteries for Catholics and Russian sailors, inmates at a girls' prison and immigrants from China. Grave sites were established in the heart of today's Financial District, in the Presidio, near Lake Merced and where locals picnic at Dolores Park today. By the late 1930s, most of these cemeteries were gone—the headstones were, anyway.

For any metropolitan area, especially one as space constrained as San Francisco, this is not unusual. In London, a series of Burial Acts were passed in the 1850s, prohibiting most interments within the city, and many graves were moved to new, large cemeteries located farther afield. But many of the deeper graves remained in the ground as buildings and parks took the place of cemeteries in central London.[3] New York has a similar history, as burials were limited and eventually relocated as the population expanded. Today, a variety of New York City buildings, including the Trump Soho Hotel and a public school, PS 60, sit on top of early settlers' graves.[4]

But no other city attempted as many removals as San Francisco did. "The removal of church and even larger city cemeteries was, indeed, fairly common, but not on the scale fairly proposed in San Francisco," writes Tamara Venit Shelton.[5] Famously, about 150,000 graves were dug up in the early to mid-1900s and moved to Colma, San Francisco's necropolis located just a few miles south of the city. Less famously, 50,000 or more were left behind, many to be forgotten and built on top of.[6]

Each person in these graves is someone who likely dreamed they would not be forgotten. They were someone's parent, child, sibling, friend, colleague. They came to San Francisco during its earliest days as a city and helped make it the beautiful and complicated place it is today. Most of those who were left behind were poor, many of them immigrants, particularly from China. They labored hard in life and weren't treated especially well. When it came time to ask the living to move their beloved dead from San Francisco to Colma, nobody came to claim these remains, either because no one local knew them or because they couldn't afford the cost.

In today's world, many people will tell you that the remains of the dead are not significant, no more than fertilizer for the soil, and yet disrespect for the dead feels deeply wrong. We are shocked and upset by the anonymous burials of women from Ciudad Juarez, Mexico, or when people's lifeless bodies are dragged through the streets. When we hear about a mass, unmarked grave,

Monument for Jennie Roosevelt Pool at Cypress Lawn Memorial Park in Colma, California. San Francisco moved more than 150,000 graves to Colma in the early twentieth century. *Seattleretro/Wikimedia Commons, licensed under the Creative Commons Attribution 3.0 Unported license.*

Celebrants at a Dia de los Muertos (Day of the Dead) Celebration in the Mission District of San Francisco, California. *Jaredzimmerman (WMF)/Wikimedia Commons, licensed under the Creative Commons Attribution-Share Alike 3.0 Unported license.*

we think of atrocities; and yet we have a few such graves right here in San Francisco. Humans are wired to see a body, a corpse, in relationship to a living person and are drawn to care for the dead in some way, even long after they're gone. It's unsettling to find out that the spot beneath our feet contains human remains, in part because we imagine that those remains belong in the separate, sacred spaces we call cemeteries and also because we can imagine being that forgotten corpse underneath a parking lot or a museum. If we believe in ghosts, it's easy to imagine that theirs must be unhappy ones.

San Francisco is a deeply multicultural city, with large populations of Mexican and Chinese people, for whom honoring the dead is a significant and active practice. Each November, Mexican families celebrate Dia de los Muertos, constructing *ofrendas* (altars) to their beloved dead, visiting their loved ones in cemeteries and forming processions through the streets of the Mission District, dressed in bright clothing and flowers with faces made up to resemble beautiful skulls. In April, Chinese families flock to cemeteries for Qingming, sweeping the graves of their ancestors and laying out elaborate feasts to share with the dead. Some return to cemeteries in the ninth month of the Chinese calendar for Chung Yeung, again to clean graves and share food. In that context, the way that many of San Francisco's indigent and immigrant dead were treated—not just being forgotten but being relocated, mixed up with other remains or treated like literal garbage, all of which happened here—looks a lot like colonialism and racism.

Before the Spanish began settling San Francisco in the late eighteenth century, the city was home to about 1,500 Ramaytush Ohlone for ten thousand years. They lived in a few communities, one near Candlestick Point, another along Mission Creek and a third near Crissy Field, and they collaborated, traded and intermarried with other tribes nearby. After the missionaries arrived, their numbers were largely wiped out. Remains of their villages and burial sites have been discovered over time as the city has been developed and redeveloped. I am not including most of those sites in this book, even though some of that information is publicly available, because I don't have the cultural background to do their stories justice.

The practice of burying the dead in graveyards is a relatively recent one; some of my own ancestors from England, Ireland and Scotland buried their most important people in walk-in tombs made from megaliths, often covered by mounds of earth. These kinds of burials appear to have been reserved for royalty, significant warriors and other wealthy elites. It's difficult to know what happened to everyone else, because their remains are long gone. Over time, even bones decompose into nothing. The Romans regularly cremated the bodies of their dead, although burials outside the city were also common. In many parts of Asia, people practiced sky burials—leaving bodies on a mountaintop or on a tall platform to decompose or be eaten by scavengers. Excarnation, a process of defleshing the bones either via scavengers or human efforts, was also widespread throughout Europe and Asia. Each came with its own set of beliefs and customs, too detailed and varied to describe here.

The word *cemetery* comes from the Greek word *koimhthrion* and its Latin counterpart *coemeterium*, meaning "a place to sleep" or "a dormitory." It was first applied to graveyards by early Christian leaders, especially once the idea of the second coming of Christ and the resurrection really took off. If Jesus was going to come back and raise everyone up, then surely they were only slumbering. For that reason, their bodies also needed to be intact and, in many cases, buried facing east, so they would be able to face the "new day" when Jesus returned. For centuries, cemeteries were attached to local churches, making the terms *churchyard* and *cemetery* practically synonymous.

San Francisco as we know it today was established during this long period when the burial of the entire body was the most common practice before embalming was popularized during and after the Civil War. From San Francisco's earliest days, settlers found places to bury the dead, either in dedicated spots like the Mission Dolores Cemetery or in "impromptu" locations, like the Sailor's Burying Ground north of the Sansome Street waterfront. Again and again, San Francisco's leaders identified burial spots they thought would remain distant from city life for decades to come, only to find it surrounded by disgruntled neighbors within a few years. No one anticipated how quickly San Francisco would grow, particularly with the lure of gold in the California hills in the 1850s. In 1794, the city's population was just 1,056. It remained low until 1849, when an estimated 90,000 people poured into California. By December 1849, San Francisco's population had ballooned to 25,000, and it continued to grow exponentially. By 1900, when residences and businesses had come to surround the city's once-remote cemeteries and locals were clamoring to evict the dead, the city's population was 342,782.[7]

San Francisco's cemetery history challenges us to think about our relationship to the settlers still buried beneath our feet. Mostly, these are not ancient dead from some early civilization. They died within the past 250 years, most of them more recently than that. Not only are they part of our city's recent history, but they are also a big part of the reason we are here today. But leaving these places unmarked means we are allowed and even encouraged to forget about them. We think of cemeteries as something we have outsourced to Colma, miles from our city limits, so we are not confronted with the realities of death and the dead unless we pass by the gravestones at Mission Dolores or the San Francisco National Cemetery on a regular basis.

But many dead are still here. You can hardly dig—either to build a patio or a public transportation hub—without finding someone's grave. The famous scene in *Poltergeist*, in which the Freeling family realizes their home is built on top of an unmarked cemetery, comes to mind. But more seriously, what does it say about San Francisco that its cemeteries were such a mess and that its grand plan to move every grave to Colma turned into a debacle? This is a city where local victims of the 1906 earthquake (3,000), the AIDS epidemic (20,000), the Jonestown massacre (900) and the COVID-19 pandemic (1,205 and counting) couldn't be buried in the place they called home. In San Francisco, do the dead matter? Time and time again, through a combination of poor planning, a lack of foresight and human greed, city officials have demonstrated that the city's dead don't matter.

I want to make sure that San Francisco's forgotten dead are remembered—to make sure living residents know they are there, both when we're strolling through parks or city streets where we've buried our dead and when we're excavating to build something new. We should include these places on maps, erect durable signs and monuments and cease pretending like they are no longer there. We have done this in a few places, but we need to apply this practice in many more. No matter how we might feel about what happens to our bodies when we die or about how our loved ones' remains are handled, we owe it to these early San Franciscans—and ourselves—to respect them.

1

CREEK OF SORROWS

MISSION DOLORES CEMETERY

F rancisca Alvarez y Nicolasa was just seven or eight years old when she died of unknown causes at the Mission San Francisco de Asís in early 1777.[8] Given her age, it's likely she died from one of several diseases circulating in Spanish-occupied California at the time: smallpox, influenza, dysentery or maybe measles. Francisca's father, Joaquin Alvarez, was a soldier with the Spanish military; her mother was María Nicolasa. They must have been devastated to lose her. But in her passing, she made a kind of history: when she was buried next to the mission church on March 4, 1777, Francisca became one of the first to be interred in the brand-new Spanish settlement.

At the time, the mission was less than six months old, and San Francisco wasn't even a small town yet. For ten thousand years before the Spanish arrived, the Ohlone people lived in small villages around the city, including near today's Presidio, Fort Mason, Crissy Field and Sutro Baths.[9] Tribespeople moved around, staying in temporary villages to hunt, fish and forage for food, and they occasionally set intentional fires to renew the land. The Chutchui and Sitlintac tribes lived among the rolling hills and beside the waterways later named Mission Creek and Arroyo de los Dolores.[10]

Their lives were turned upside down in late 1769, when Sergeant José Ortega, sailing under the command of Spanish military leader Gaspár de Portolá, sighted the Golden Gate and the San Francisco Bay. At the same time, Spanish missionaries with the Franciscan Order, under the leadership

A painting of Ohlone people rowing a tule boat on the San Francisco Bay. *Louis Choris/ Wikimedia Commons, public domain.*

of Father Junipero Serra, began scouting for sites across California to build a series of missions in an effort to convert the indigenous people of the state to Catholicism.[11] They built the first mission in San Diego, called the Mission San Diego El Alcalá, in 1769. Missions sprang up in Carmel in 1770, in San Gabriel and a remote part of Monterey County in 1771 and in San Luis Obispo in 1772.

San Francisco was next. Even before the official mission was built, a temporary structure opened at the present-day corner of Albion and Camp Streets. Father Francisco Palou, a fifty-three-year-old Franciscan born in Majorca, Spain, led the inaugural mass on June 27, 1776, about a week before the United States Congress adopted the Declaration of Independence. San Francisco's permanent mission church, now the oldest surviving structure in San Francisco, was dedicated on August 2, 1791.[12]

The mission's formal name—Mission San Francisco de Asís—comes from St. Francis of Assisi. He founded the Franciscan order that built and ran California's chain of twenty-one missions. (It's likely that Francisca, the first girl buried here, was named after him.) But its nickname, Mission Dolores, comes from a nearby creek, the Arroyo de los Dolores, or "Creek of Sorrows." Local Ohlone called the waterway Ehwate, but the Spanish explorers, possibly Juan Bautista de Anza or a fellow traveler, Father Pedro

V. R. DEL V. P. F. JUNIPERO SERRA

An illustration showing Junípero Serra holding a crucifix in one hand and a stone in the other, preaching to a crowd of indigenous people. *From Francisco Palou,* Francisco Palou's Life and Apostolic Labors of the Venerable Father Junípero Serra, Founder of the Franciscan Missions of California, *with an introduction and notes by George Wharton James (Pasadena, CA: G.W. James, 1913).*

Font, renamed it.[13] "We arrived at a beautiful creek, which, because it was Friday of Sorrows, we called the Arroyo de Los Dolores," they later wrote.

For the Ohlone, Miwok and other indigenous people in the region, the mission quickly became a place of sorrows. In the process of "converting" indigenous people to Catholicism, the Franciscans came close to eliminating tribal peoples and their cultures, lands and spiritual practices. Chamis, a twenty-year-old Ohlone man who lived in the Chutchui village, became the first indigenous adult to be baptized at Mission Dolores on June 24, 1777, just a few months after Francisca Alvarez y Nicolasa's burial. He was renamed Francisco Moraga. His future wife, Paszém, was baptized and renamed Catarina de Bononia. They were married in a Catholic ceremony at the Mission Dolores on April 24, 1778. Many others were baptized, renamed and Christianized. The Franciscans did everything they could to erase these people's culture, origins and family ties.

The Mission Dolores became a village unto itself, with herds of livestock for food, farms for growing fruits and vegetables, and everything else a settlement needs to keep going. Although the mission leaders promised to preserve indigenous people's lands and baptism was supposedly voluntary, tribespeople were worked very hard: building mission structures, tending farmlands and doing much of the labor of daily mission life. They also built the permanent mission structures, which were made out of adobe (a mixture of earth, straw and dung), starting in 1783.[14] The relentless labor proved to be too much. An indigenous man named Charquín led the first band of runaways in 1789, and in the summer of 1795, 280 people abandoned the mission due to "too much work, too much punishment and too much hunger," according to Brother Guire Cleary. Measles, smallpox and diphtheria regularly swept through the mission, as did syphilis and bacterial infections, killing hundreds.

In response, the Franciscan order opened the Mission San Rafael Arcángel nineteen miles to the north in December 1817.[15] It was founded as a hospital for sick indigenous people and named for Raphael, the archangel of healing. San Francisco's cold, foggy weather made it a poor place to recuperate from the illnesses that ravaged the indigenous population at Mission Dolores, but the warmer weather at Mission San Rafael seemed to help some of them heal. It wasn't enough to save the many thousands of others who remained, died and were buried in San Francisco.

"By 1810, more than 5,000 years of tribal life in the Bay Area had effectively ended," Cleary wrote. They were by no means wiped out—many of their descendants live in and around San Francisco today, carrying on

An early sketch of the Mission San Francisco de Asís (Mission Dolores) at Mission and Sixteenth Streets in San Francisco, date unknown. *Historic American Buildings Survey, Library of Congress.*

or reclaiming the Ohlone language and traditions. But the arrival of the missionaries shattered their way of life, all in the name of "saving souls" (and forced labor). An estimated 5,500 indigenous people of the San Francisco Bay Area were buried in and around the Mission Dolores Cemetery, but if you visited the place now, you'd hardly know it.

The mission's churchyard was the first official burial ground for European settlers in San Francisco. In the years between Francisca's burial in 1777 and the final burial, that of 106-year-old Clorinde Castillo in 1953, between ten thousand and eleven thousand people were laid to rest here. Unlike many others buried in San Francisco's cemeteries, most of them remain here.[16]

As visitors emerge from the mission buildings and enter the churchyard, they are greeted by a tomb with low walls made of worn brick and an A-frame structure of iron, rusty with age. Several headstones, some intact and many more chipped or broken and repaired, cluster around the tomb, many of them carved with Irish names. For decades, this was San Francisco's only Catholic cemetery, and dozens of the city's Irish immigrants were laid to rest here.

The churchyard is laid out in tidy rows with concrete paths that wind among the headstones. Several mature trees shade the small burial ground, including a massive palm and a towering redwood that's many decades old. Rose bushes planted among the graves are tended weekly by the Golden

The Mission Dolores Cemetery with the mission buildings in the background, date unknown. *Historic American Buildings Survey, Library of Congress.*

Gate Rose Society, and local birds dart among succulents, rosemary, ivy, manzanita and bear's breeches, whose leaves can be crushed to help heal wounds and burns.

Standing in this small churchyard, it's hard to imagine that thousands of graves lie below the surface. Only about two hundred headstones remain, mainly bearing the names of the powerful Spanish families who settled San Francisco and the Irish immigrants who arrived seeking opportunities and gold. Among the dead here are Luis Antonio Arguello, the state's first Mexican governor; Lieutenant Gabriel Moraga, the first commandant of the Presidio; Don Francisco De Haro, the first alcalde (mayor) of San Francisco; and William Leidesdorff, one of the first biracial (Black) U.S. citizens and a powerful businessman in San Francisco's earliest days.

Mission Dolores remained the only Catholic cemetery in San Francisco until Calvary Cemetery was established on Lone Mountain in the 1850s. But getting to the mission for a burial was not easy; "a funeral procession from the heart of the town to Mission Dolores graveyard, moving through sand dunes and across marshes and swamps, consumed most of a day," Michael Svanevik and Shirley Burgess write in *City of Souls.*[17]

Once a township unto itself, Mission Dolores was eventually abandoned. The mission period in California ended in 1833, and in 1834, Mission Dolores was ordered to be turned over to an administrator. By the mid-1850s, the mission buildings were beginning to crumble and fall apart.

But burials kept going, even as the area around Mission Dolores became an entertainment outpost for people who lived and worked in downtown San Francisco.[18] Over time, more locals began making their homes in the neighborhood, and the pressures of urban expansion forced the mission's and cemetery's footprints to shrink. Mission Dolores lands once extended far beyond the site's current boundaries, and the churchyard was, at its peak, three times its current one-third-of-an-acre size. Although the cemetery is one of the few in San Francisco that was allowed to preserve some of its burials within city limits, it still suffered at the hands of development and expansion.

In late April 1888, several property owners urged the San Francisco Street Committee to pay for the cost of expanding Sixteenth Street, essentially lopping off the north side of the mission property. But there was a problem: a number of burials were located right where the proposed extension would

The Mission Dolores Cemetery viewed from the street in 1868. *Historic American Buildings Survey, Library of Congress.*

go. City leaders estimated that buying the land from the mission would cost $5,000, and it would cost another $2,000 to remove the bodies.[19] In September that year, the city passed a resolution to take just $2,000 from the Street Department fund to open Sixteenth Street.[20]

By the end of May 1889, most of the four hundred to five hundred graves located on the north side of Mission Dolores, where Sixteenth Street would go, had been dug up and moved, but a handful remained, pending the approval of the San Francisco Board of Supervisors.[21] More were removed by mid-June, "with the exception of two, which will be kept there until the money is paid," according to a reporter for the *Daily Alta California*, who did not divulge the names of those buried.[22] This morbid hostage situation ultimately worked: four days after that article was published, the Street Committee finally agreed to pay Mission Dolores's archbishop, Patrick Riordan, $2,000 "for the city's share of the expense of removing the bodies…which obstruct the opening of Sixteenth Street."[23]

These graves were quite old, and the remains were handled as carefully as possible. "Three bodies disinterred yesterday were found beneath the roots of cypress trees that had been planted upward of thirty years ago," a *Morning Call* reporter wrote.

> *In every instance, except two or three recent interments, there was nothing to be found except a few bones, or badly corroded coffin plates. These, as a rule, were placed in new boxes. There was no mixing of bodies. When they were unknown, a simple cross marks the place of reinterment, upon which is inscribed 'unknown,' or sometimes the number of the lot or grave from which they were taken. This, however, has seldom been necessary as most of the remains were localized by a slab or tablet.[24]*

The majority of these graves, 446 of them, were relocated to another part of the Mission Dolores Cemetery, according to the *San Francisco Morning Call*. The rest were scattered across the city and beyond: ten went to Calvary Cemetery on Lone Mountain, forty went to Holy Cross in Colma, the remains of a member of the Peralta family went to Oakland, the remains of someone named Murphy went to Vallejo and the remains of two children were reinterred at Odd Fellows Cemetery, also on Lone Mountain.[25]

A similar scene unfolded in November 1889, when property owners along Dolores Street asked the board of supervisors to spend $1,500 to widen the street in front of the mission. At the time, the cemetery extended beyond the front of the mission church—after all, it had been there long before any streets were laid out. "The matter was laid over until there is money available for the purpose," a *Daily Alta California* reporter wrote. In the meantime, the supervisors asked the mission to convey the land in question to the city.[26] In July 1890, the city's health officer began issuing permits to remove the dead in that portion of the cemetery, after which "the fence will be set back, and Dolores Street opened to its full width."[27] As far as we know, that's what ultimately happened.

But it appears that the burials behind the current Mission Dolores property and the current churchyard fence were handled very differently. According to research compiled by John Blackett, the city told families it would pay to remove headstones but not the bodies, and many families couldn't afford to have the remains of their loved ones dug up and buried elsewhere. Thousands of burials, including 5,515 burials of indigenous people, are now sealed beneath a layer of asphalt, where the children of Mission Dolores Academy play at recess and lunch.[28] Occasionally, as the pavement settles, cracks reveal the outlines of coffins still resting beneath the ground.

Almost half of all Americans, 46 percent, believe ghosts are real in some form.[29] Paranormal investigators debate whether ghosts are the literal spirits of the dead or memories somehow recorded in the landscape of a place, looping again and again like an on-hold recording. People who are sensitive to ghosts and hauntings often report sensing the spirits of the dead—or even spotting ghosts—when they visit graveyards like the one at Mission Dolores.

In March 1891, a *Morning Call* reporter toured the Mission Dolores Cemetery with a local police officer, who asked him as they entered the derelict grounds, "Do you believe in ghosts?" The reporter didn't reply but laughed a little. The officer said, "Well, if you are not afraid of ghosts, at least take a care to your steps as I am leading you into a place that has gone to decay."

Stepping from Dolores Street into the burial ground was a bit like traveling between the present and the past, the reporter wrote. Outside, Dolores Street was lined with "fine stone walks, a well-laid cobble-stone gutter and graded street." Inside, he found dozens of open, unfilled graves and, deeper inside, "an undergrowth that chokes up and hides from view many of the stones that mark the last home of so many people."

Eventually, the officer revealed why he asked about ghosts. One night, while walking into the churchyard to visit his uncle's grave, "my hat struck against the overhanging branches of a weeping willow. I felt a thrill travel down my body, my heart paused in terror, my hat left its place and my hair seemed to bristle with electricity. I was scared for the second time, then I had

A reconstructed Ohlone hut at Mission Dolores that was built by Andrew Galvan, an Ohlone man and the Old Mission's curator. *Ed Bierman/Wikimedia Commons, licensed under the Creative Commons Attribution 2.0 Generic license.*

to laugh. I thought a thousand things in a second, yet I didn't think at all, for I seemed to comprehend all the terrors in existence," he said.

As they walked around, the reporter lamented that the graves of rich and poor, powerful and powerless alike were falling into decay. In his article, he wished the city and the cemetery's neighbors would take better care of a place they might be buried in someday.

In some ways, he got his wish. Today, the Mission Dolores Cemetery, along with the original church building, is in much better shape. A new basilica was constructed on the property in 1918, and it has hosted religious services regularly since then. The older church, built of adobe, survived the 1906 earthquake and fire with minimal damage and was restored in 1917. Today, the original mission and cemetery function as a kind of history museum, maintained through ticket sales and volunteer upkeep. The cemetery is well-tended and scattered with benches for visitors to sit and reflect.

A life-sized statue of Father Junipero Serra stands at the center of the cemetery, sculpted by Arthur Putnam in 1918.[30] But the churchyard also features a replica of an Ohlone hut constructed from dried golden tule grass. It was built by Andrew Galvan, a local Ohlone/Miwok man and the Old Mission's curator, as a "kind of a get-back," he told the *Storied: San Francisco* podcast. "Most cultures in California are building houses on top of our old, ancient cemeteries. So, I built an Ohlone house on top of an invader cemetery."[31]

A statue of Kateri Tekakwitha also stands among the Mission Dolores gravestones. She was a Mohawk woman who survived smallpox in the late seventeenth century, was converted to Catholicism and remained a virgin until her death in 1680, when she was twenty-four. She achieved sainthood in 2012. The pedestal that supports her statue reads, "In prayerful memory of the faithful Indians."[32] Although the Mission Dolores of today acknowledges the work, deaths and burials of so many indigenous people on the property, it still doesn't completely own up to the ways it harmed Bay Area tribes.

2

GUARDIANS OF THE DEAD

SAN FRANCISCO'S CYPRESS TREES

In ancient Greece, there once lived a handsome boy named Cyparissus, and his most beloved companion was a stag. This stag was tame, friendly and kind; it would visit people's homes and reach out its neck, even to strangers, hoping to be petted.[33]

One scorching summer day, the stag lay down in the shade to rest and soak up the coolness of the earth. Somehow—the details are vague—Cyparissus stabbed the stag with his javelin, killing it. When he saw what he had done, he "resolved to die himself," begging the gods that he should be allowed to mourn forever. They answered him by transforming him into a cypress tree. The god Apollo, seeing this, said, "I shall mourn for you… while you yourself will mourn for others and be the constant companion for those in distress."[34]

Today, cypress trees are associated with cemeteries and memorials for the dead around the world. They're often called churchyard cypresses because they are so often found in and around graveyards. Historically, some people associated cypress trees with the underworld because they didn't grow back well when they were pruned too severely. In Greece, grieving households were decked with boughs of cypress, and cypress branches were used to fumigate the air during cremations.

Northern California is home to a separate breed of cypress trees, the Monterey cypress, or *Cupressus macrocarpa*, sometimes called the coast cypress for its tendency to grow along the wild bluffs of the California shore. While the cypress trees of classical Greece—*Cupressus sempervirens*—grow in narrow,

Cypress trees at Lincoln Park Golf Course, the location of City Cemetery, San Francisco's largest public cemetery. *Beth Winegarner.*

conical shapes, the Monterey cypress grows irregularly and is often flat on top due to its exposure to fierce winds off the Pacific. These trees often look like they're frozen in the middle of a hurricane.

San Francisco's cemeteries are often marked by Monterey cypress trees. Even though City Cemetery, near Land's End, reportedly contained no trees when it was established in the 1860s, it is ringed with tall cypress trees today. For an extra aesthetic touch, many are draped in Spanish moss. A lone cypress leans out over the street on the peak of Russian Hill, which got its name from an early burial ground for Russian sailors. Cypress trees shade the gardens at the Lone Mountain campus of the University of San Francisco, a hilltop once surrounded by 170 acres of burial grounds. And mature cypress trees watch over the dead in Mission Dolores's churchyard, where some of the city's first settlers were buried.

Granted, cypress trees are among San Francisco's most common trees. They don't make very good street trees; they grow much too large, topping out near one hundred feet tall with a trunk at least a couple of feet in diameter.[35] But they're often found in the area's backyards and city parks. And as it happens, some of San Francisco's parks were once burial grounds. There's no public census on how many cypress trees there are in San

Francisco. Despite being poor street trees, almost 1,900 of them are planted along local streets, including 1,639 Monterey cypress trees.[36] Local cypress trees were commonly planted in the late 1800s as the city was developing its park system, and they have become an accidental and subversive reminder of what places like Lincoln Park, Dolores Park and Lone Mountain used to be. If you visit any of these former cemeteries, keep an eye out. More than likely, cypress trees will be standing sentinel, companions for those in distress, like Cyparissus with his fallen stag.

3

"IMPROMPTU BURIALS"

SAN FRANCISCO'S EARLY UNOFFICIAL CEMETERIES

The Mission Dolores Cemetery served as San Francisco's only settler cemetery for five decades, and it was a perfectly good place to be buried—as long as you were Catholic. For that half a century, it seemed as though the Spanish missionaries, along with their military protectors at the Presidio, might be the only ones interested in settling on this small, sandy, swampy peninsula. But that began to change in 1835, when whaler and entrepreneur William Richardson built the first homestead outside the Mission Dolores area, near where Washington and Kearny Streets intersect today. Soon after, Richardson began laying out plans for the surrounding streets. He named the new bayside village Yerba Buena, after the mint-like herb that grew abundantly in the city.[37]

More European settlers trickled in, including about 240 Mormons, who arrived from the East Coast in July 1846. That summer, the population of Yerba Buena was around 500, and obviously not all of them were Catholic. Many of the city's early cemeteries were pretty informal; locals picked a spot that seemed good for burial and began digging graves there. But with the gold rush, that changed quickly. Thousands of people began pouring into the city.

Many newcomers "were weakened and sick from their long sea voyage and never got nearer to the mines than this. Others came down from the mines, discouraged and worn out physically, and succumbed to the city's fog and cold," writes Helen Marcia Bruner.[38] She continues:

A sketch of a mining camp in California after the discovery of gold in 1849. *Flickr's "The Commons," public domain.*

Tents were the usual shelter and sometimes there were not enough of them or the price for lodging in them could not be met. These people were all strangers to one another and busy with their own affairs. One writer says it was not an unusual sight to see a body under a clump of bushes, no one knowing or caring whose it was, and no one taking the trouble to bury it decently. If one of the lodgers in a tent died, his fellow lodgers often dug a hole in the sand nearby and buried him there as quickly as possible.

Some of these burials were uncovered in the decades that followed, as workers graded the streets, sunk wells and dug foundations for new homes. Occasionally, these bodies might have been moved to San Francisco's first municipal cemetery, Yerba Buena, which opened in 1850. But most of them were probably built over, writes San Francisco archaeologist Kari Hervey-Lentz.[39]

While many early settlers were buried alone or in small groups, a few spots around the city took in dozens or even hundreds of graves. One of the earliest graveyards was located just west of Telegraph Hill, and it was forgotten almost as soon as it was created.

SAILOR'S BURYING GROUND

(Sansome Street Cemetery, Telegraph Hill Cemetery)

It's unclear how James Anderson, a native of Canterbury, England, wound up aboard the USF *Congress*, a frigate headed for San Francisco. The three-masted *Congress* was first launched in 1841, and by the mid-1840s, it was patrolling the West Coast of the United States during the Mexican-American War. Ship life was rough: cramped living quarters, rationed food and rampant infection and disease, including typhus, smallpox and tuberculosis. Anderson didn't survive his time aboard the warship; he died on July 16, 1847, of unknown causes. When the *Congress* next docked in San Francisco, Anderson's comrades buried his remains in the city's ad-hoc Sailor's Burying Ground near the corner of Sansome Street and Broadway. Back then, before early San Franciscans filled in the shoreline, the graveyard was essentially on the waterfront.

Anderson wasn't alone; fifteen to twenty other seamen from the *Congress* and *Savannah*, who died of varying causes while sailing, were buried here between 1825 and 1847. The burial ground, sometimes called the Telegraph Hill or Sansome Street Cemetery, ultimately took in about eighty to one hundred graves. Many belonged to seamen, "whalers and hide droghers [traders]," the *Daily Alta California* reported. Others buried there included two sailors from a whaling vessel that came to San Francisco for a refit and, for a brief period, Eliab Grimes, a wealthy sea merchant whose remains were later moved to Honolulu.[40] But it also became a resting place for Protestants, Jews, Greeks and others who could not be buried at Mission Dolores.

Walking around this gently sloping block today, you wouldn't know it was once hallowed ground. A four-story building with a nondescript ground-level parking garage now occupies the block, its columns of dark-gray brick divided by large, identical windows. One of San Francisco's broadcast news channels, KPIX, operates from this building, as does a local AM radio station KCBS, which plays nothing but news around the clock. The waterfront is still nearby, but it's now a few blocks away, rather than lapping at the borders of the cemetery.

Between the mid-1820s and the mid-1840s, the Sailor's Burying Ground was on a remote slope overlooking the San Francisco Bay, separated from the village downtown by rolling, tree-dotted hills. But by 1847, even before the gold rush, city officials were planning San Francisco's expansion. As they prepared to build the public highway that would become Broadway, an article in the

A view of Vallejo Street and the San Francisco Bay from Sansome Street, where the Sailor's Burying Ground once lay, taken between 1860 and 1870. *Lawrence & Houseworth (publisher), Library of Congress.*

San Francisco Californian asked authorities to show some respect for the burials on the property. "We hope…that our Alcalde will give the subject his earliest consideration, and select a more suitable place, for the *burial of the dead*."[41]

It's unclear whether any burials were moved at that time, but it seems unlikely. There wasn't anywhere to move them; San Francisco's first official public cemetery, the Yerba Buena Cemetery at Larkin and Market Streets, didn't open until 1850. The Sailor's Burying Ground, it seems, was forgotten until 1857. That January, a rainstorm kicked off an avalanche of rocks and dirt that exposed several coffins, as well as a headboard—that is, a grave marker made from wood—with information on the seamen buried there, including James Anderson.[42] San Francisco's coroner "took charge of the coffins and bones exposed" by the landslide and intended to move them to a more appropriate spot.

A few days later, however, as workmen were taking stone from Telegraph Hill for ballast, they discovered even more remains. Their treatment of the situation was less respectful than the coroner's: "It is said also that as the stone is taken away, pieces of the coffins, as they are dug out, and the remains they contain, are taken with the stone and carried on board the ships to be ballasted," a *Stockton Daily Argus* reporter wrote.[43] They continued, "This is scarcely Christian decency. The graves of these early pioneers, who came to California before the magic charm of gold allured us hither, who came here in the service of their country, and who died while serving it, ought not to be desecrated in this manner, and some little degree of respect is due them."

Even then, it doesn't appear that all the graves were moved. A *Daily Alta California* article from 1858 reports, "The matter came before the city authorities, but nothing was done towards having them taken up and elsewhere interred."[44] A day earlier, workmen again were shoveling ballast in the cemetery when an embankment collapsed, and a human skeleton rattled down with it. "The laborers, who were ignorant of the use to which the place had formerly been put, stood aghast, and one or two made a stampede from the locality," the reporter wrote.

The graves at the Sailor's Burying Ground may have ultimately been moved to Yerba Buena Cemetery, according to the folks at SF Genealogy.[45] If so, it wasn't much of a final rest either. By 1858, Yerba Buena was already falling into serious disrepair and being urged to move its burials elsewhere. Some of San Francisco's earliest dead were moved multiple times, a pattern that has come to define the city's relationship to its settlers and builders.

"IMPROMPTU BURIALS"

Before 1850, many vacant lots in the eastern part of San Francisco were "used for impromptu burials."[46] These included the Sailor's Burying Ground and graveyards on Russian Hill, in North Beach, at First and Minna Streets, and elsewhere. Looking back, it's easy to criticize those early settlers' lack of foresight, their inability to predict that Yerba Buena Village would soon become a lively urban area. But downtown San Francisco in those days was very different, full of tall sand dunes and swampland, difficult to traverse on foot or by horse. Maybe it was impossible to imagine that more than a few hundred people would want to live in this windy, foggy place, let alone that it might become an intensely compact, world-class city.

Montgomery Street (named after John Montgomery, the U.S. Naval officer who raised the American flag over San Francisco in 1846) was home to at least two ad-hoc cemeteries. One was located on the block bordered today by Bush, Montgomery, Pine and Sansome Streets. Another was just a half block away, bounded by Montgomery, Leidesdorff and California Streets; its southern border was about halfway between California and Pine Streets. At the time, Montgomery Street probably hadn't been graded yet, and it, too, was right on the waterfront of San Francisco Bay. Little is known about these two cemeteries, including when they saw their first burials or how many were interred at either spot. The graves were later (allegedly) moved to Yerba Buena Cemetery.[47]

Today, these sites are in the heart of downtown San Francisco. Instead of headstones, they now house architectural landmarks, including the historic Mills building, which was built in 1892 and restored after the 1906

Montgomery Street in 1866, not long after two early cemeteries were uprooted nearby. *Lawrence & Houseworth (publisher), Library of Congress.*

earthquake, and the Pacific Stock Exchange building, with its ornate columns and Art Deco sculptures.

A third unofficial burial ground, sometimes called Happy Valley, was located along First Street between Minna and Natoma Streets and extended most of the way to Second Street.[48] It likely operated in the 1840s and maybe into the 1850s but was soon forgotten. In the 1890s, workmen found skeleton after skeleton as they excavated the site for the construction of a four-story brick building.

At first, they thought they might have discovered evidence of a murder, but as more remains surfaced, the workers, supervised by Edward Haaf of Haaf and Dunphy, realized they had a cemetery on their hands. A reporter wrote for the *San Francisco Call* in February 1894:

> *The shovel of one struck upon a skull. Bit by bit the other bones of the human anatomy were laid bare amid the debris of what might have been a rude coffin. Presently another similar discovery was made and then another. None of the bodies were deeper than two and a half feet below the surface. In all, six bodies were reported at one time, and Mr. Haaf said that there were evidences of more being in the neighborhood. One skeleton still wore the blue pantaloons associated with military attire.*[49]

The city coroner confirmed that these remains had been "regularly interred." As the bones were unearthed, they were stuffed into a wooden barrel before the coroner took them away.

The discovery attracted quite a crowd of onlookers, including an elderly citizen, Robert Gunn, who had lived at First and Minna Streets since September 1851 and remembered seeing headboards set up to mark the graves of early settlers. "He remembered the interment there of a child of Mr. Hall, a grocery-dealer doing business at what is now Lick Alley and First Street. 'Minna was a fashionable street in those days, viz., in '51.' said Mr. Gunn. 'Captain John Egan, Philip A. Roach, General Richardson, ex-Sheriff Doane of the Vigilance Committee. White, the big lumberman, Bert McNulty and many other notables lived down there, and there may be hundreds of graves in the plat,'" wrote the reporter for the *Call*. Bruner put the number closer to seventy-five.[50]

Over the years, graves turned up again and again on the Happy Valley Cemetery site, including the bones of an adult and child in 1865, four more graves during Haaf's work in 1894, a skeleton in a coffin in 1902 and another complete skeleton in 1937.[51] The 1902 find occurred as two boys

Stockton Street as seen from Market Street sometime between 1860 and 1870. The building on the right sits on the site of an early cemetery. *Lawrence & Houseworth (publisher), Library of Congress.*

were playing in an excavation site near Second and Minna Streets. They jumped on a redwood board they discovered sticking out of the wet sand. It shattered, revealing a coffin containing a human skeleton. "The bones were black with age and were loose, all the ligaments and the shroud in which the body had been enveloped having rotted away."[52]

The remains found in 1894 were removed to the city morgue and reinterred in City Cemetery, the city's municipal cemetery from 1870 to 1900. But many more may yet remain in the ground, close to the city's new multistory Transbay Transit Center and Salesforce Park, as well as the record-breaking Salesforce Tower.

Yet another, perhaps more official, public cemetery was established at the corner of Stockton and Market Streets, according to a July 1853 article in the *Daily Alta California*.[53] By the time that article appeared, the burial ground was in shambles: "Its present exposed condition, and frequent attempts at the desecration of the graves, renders the appointment of a Watchman necessary, and that a fence should at once be erected around so much of the grounds as are at present occupied. At the junction of Stockton and Market streets, several graves have been discovered, and the bodies exposed. It of course is only necessary to call attention to the matter to have it remedied," a reporter wrote. It's astonishing that city officials might not collect and reinter the remains on their own without the prompting of the local press. Then again, San Francisco barely had a leadership structure in place at that time. Recently, the spot was occupied by a Forever 21 fast fashion store and serves as a gateway to the Union Square shopping district.

Another early cemetery was established on Rincon Point, where the Infinity condominium building is today, on Folsom Street between Main and Spear Streets. At the time, Rincon Point was a narrow spit of land jutting into San Francisco Bay, surrounded on three sides by water and reserved for use by the U.S. government. This graveyard was connected to the U.S. Marine Hospital that opened on Rincon Point in 1853.[54] The four-story hospital had

The U.S. Marine Hospital at Spear and Harrison Streets. The hospital, which had its own cemetery for patients, closed after an earthquake in 1868. *Historic American Buildings Survey, Library of Congress.*

room for five hundred patients and boasted fantastic views of "the entire city on the North, the beautiful town of Oakland on the east, in the distance the Mission Dolores, and on the North, embraced by the waters of the Bay, Goat [Angel] and Alcatraz Islands. Daily admissions, 6; deaths per month, 4; average number of patients, 150." A violent earthquake centered across the bay in Hayward damaged the hospital in 1868, and a replacement was opened in San Francisco's Presidio in 1875. Some researchers believe that the Rincon Point graves moved there when the new hospital established a cemetery of its own, but it's difficult to be certain.

And in these early days, some people were buried in random spots or on their own property. In February 1863, some boys who were playing in a vacant lot on the north side of Washington Street, between Mason and Taylor Streets, discovered one end of what turned out to be a metal casket. Someone called the coroner's office, which sent a wagon and workmen to exhume the casket. It was engraved with the deceased's name and other information: "Henry Montgomery, Died Nov. 18th, 1850, Aged 24 years." They could tell that Henry had had smallpox but could not determine if that was what had killed him.[55]

San Francisco's northeastern neighborhoods are dotted with many early burial grounds, but one in particular marks the transition from the impromptu interments of the city's early years to the more official burials in places designated for laying loved ones to rest.

North Beach Cemetery

In 1847, a man named Anderson—his first name is lost to history—died in San Francisco of unknown causes. He was an officer in the New York Volunteer Regiment who came to the city sometime in the 1840s, when it remained a wild and sparsely populated place. Even so, he made enough friends that after his death, likely under a blanket of July fog, his comrades formed a processional up Powell Street and buried him with military honors in a graveyard bordered by today's Powell, Stockton, Filbert and Greenwich Streets. At the time, the grounds were "far from the city, where it was thought the rude hand of speculation would never disturb his mouldering remains" and where "the music of the surging waves…sung a daily requiem o'er his grave," a *Daily Alta California* reporter wrote in February 1851.[56] Standing on this block 175 years later, surrounded by the rumble and clank of North

Saints Peter and Paul Church as seen from Washington Square. The church was built on the grounds of the former North Beach Cemetery. *Christoph Radtke/Wikimedia Commons, licensed under the Creative Commons Attribution 3.0 Unported license.*

Beach's cafés, restaurants and delivery trucks, it's hard to imagine what those early San Franciscans were thinking.

Anderson may have been one of the first to be buried in this cemetery, known alternately as the North Beach Cemetery, the Powell Street Cemetery or—to that *Alta* reporter—"the Old Cemetery," but he wasn't the last. Over the next few years, as San Francisco's population exploded, eight hundred to nine hundred of the city's gold rush dead were buried on this plot of land across from Washington Square.

This was no tidy, modern cemetery, and it sounds like the cemetery's caretakers, if there were any, struggled to keep up with the number of dead who needed burial. "Body disposal was haphazard at best. Grounds weren't enclosed. Graves were heedlessly prepared. Those passing [by] could not escape the putrid odor. Sheep grazed the grounds," according to Michael Svanevik and Shirley Burgess.[57]

The population boom that quickly filled the cemetery also brought roads and housing to the neighborhood, once thought to be too remote to be disturbed by "the rude hand of speculation." As land around the burial ground became more valuable, a property owner laid claim to it. But there was a problem: the graves still weren't being maintained, and nobody wanted to live next door to a charnel pit. "A visit to this place of sepulture is sufficient to shock the sensibilities of men inured even to the battle-field rude burial of the dead," the *Alta* reported in March 1850.[58]

The newspaper urged the city to find a better spot for a cemetery, but a year later, the situation hadn't improved. "The grave of the nameless stranger is trodden under foot, streets are being cut through the cemetery, and that holiest of all earthly spots has been desecrated," the *Alta* reported in 1851.

Plans to extend Powell Street, which previously stopped below the southern edge of the cemetery, forced the issue. The city's official cemetery, Yerba Buena, had opened to the public, giving San Francisco somewhere to move the bodies interred in North Beach. City officials paid $3,000 to a contractor, W.W. Walker, to exhume and move the graves. But in February 1853, the *Daily Alta California* reported that Walker's subcontractor, a man named Fitzpatrick, was doing a horrendous job. Not all the burials had been exhumed, and those that were had been "pitched into heaps by the roadside," shoveled into carts and driven off with no effort to keep people's remains separate or identifiable. The decaying coffins were burned, while those in good condition—as well as the fence and markers around the graves—were sold for firewood or fencing.[59]

The article speculated that Fitzpatrick's checkered background, including the fact that he was a "foreigner" who'd been charged with attacking and threatening to kill another man, might explain why he was disrespecting the remains of the city's early settlers.

The newspaper followed up in May 1853, reporting again that North Beach burials had been "treated as though they were little better than carrion." Walker and Fitzpatrick's workers had left many graves behind in the "relocation" process. Henry Meiggs, a local real estate speculator who built a wharf on the waterfront where Pier 39 and Fisherman's Wharf are today, stepped in to make things right. Meiggs paid an unknown sum out of his own pocket to have the rest of the North Beach remains dug up, placed in new coffins and moved. He also paid for the grading of Powell Street, the reporter noted.[60] Unfortunately, Meiggs's real estate dealings left him broke. He committed fraud in an effort to raise money and fled in 1854 to Chile, where he became a successful railroad builder. Eventually, he paid back all the money he had fraudulently raked in.

Today, this former cemetery is in the heart of North Beach. At the center of the block is Saints Peter and Paul Church, a Catholic church that was built in 1884, originally at Filbert Street and Grant Avenue. It was rebuilt on the former cemetery site in 1924 after the 1906 earthquake and now sits at the hair-raising address of 666 Filbert Street. Its spires rise 191 feet into the North Beach sky, and its ornate stone façade features a quote from Dante's *Paradiso*: "The glory of him who moves all things penetrates and flows throughout the universe."

Russian Hill Cemetery

At the peak of Russian Hill, on the corner of Green and Jones Streets, sits a twenty-five-story building designed by famed architect Joseph Eichler and built in the mid-1960s.[61] It houses 112 condos, all of which likely boast stunning views of San Francisco and the bay. (They'd better, as the most expensive condo in the building, a combination of three units, was sold in 2017 for $6.8 million.) Its neighbor, just down the block at 947 Green Street, sports richly carved archways, a fountain and a private drive leading to condos that sell for upwards of $3 million. But a short walk down this narrow, wooded street leads to a small, steep park studded with mature trees, including maples and purple-leafed plums. A stairway passes through this tiny woodland, allowing more working-class folks to enjoy the leafy canopy next door to luxury housing. Beneath it all lies a former cemetery.

In 1848, a Russian warship anchored in San Francisco, where several of its crew were stricken with "some malarian disease." Many died. Because they could not be buried with the Catholics at Mission Dolores or the Protestants in other burial grounds, their remains were buried at a new cemetery between Taylor and Jones Streets, north of Vallejo Street.[62]

Local historians estimate that between the 1840s and 1850, thirty to forty people were buried in this plot, which featured a Russian-style cross. Russian Hill got its name from these burials and the cross that memorialized them. However, because of its steep slopes, the location was difficult for funeral corteges to reach, and burials there ceased by 1850. The *Daily Alta California* reported in June 1861 that the graves on Russian Hill had never been disturbed, but by late 1878, the remains had been removed to "other localities," according to the *San Francisco Daily Evening Post*.[63] It's possible they

Russian Hill, the site of an early Russian cemetery, as seen from the corner of Mason and Sacramento Streets. *Lawrence & Houseworth (publisher), Library of Congress.*

went to the city's Greco-Russian Cemetery, located near Lone Mountain, which opened in the 1870s, or to City Cemetery.

Walk through any of these areas now, and you wouldn't know so many early San Francisco settlers were buried here. Without major excavation work, it's impossible to know whether every grave was moved elsewhere. What's clear is that many of these early cemeteries didn't last long—maybe twenty to thirty years at most. As the gold rush arrived in San Francisco, city officials got more serious about creating appropriate places to bury the dead, but their ability to predict the future, particularly the rapid expansion of the city, didn't get any better.

4

THE HEART OF THE CITY

YERBA BUENA AND GREEN OAK CEMETERIES

James Marshall changed California history forever when he found traces of gold at Sutter's Mill in Coloma, California, 130 miles east of San Francisco. The discovery brought floods of people to California and its City by the Bay. In 1846, when San Francisco became a United States territory, about two hundred people lived in this small town. In 1849, San Francisco's population hovered around one thousand. But by 1852, its population had exploded to thirty-six thousand.[64] This rapid growth led many people to live in cramped, unsanitary conditions, whether in tents or other dwellings, and San Francisco didn't have any real hospitals or a formalized system of healthcare. Several deadly diseases, including cholera, malaria, yellow fever, typhoid, smallpox and scurvy, rampaged through the city's population.[65] One doctor estimated that between 1851 and 1853, 20 percent of the people who came to California seeking gold died within six months of their arrival.[66]

In 1850 alone, more than 1,000 people died in San Francisco, including nearly 100 aboard ships arriving in the city.[67] Some 250 to 300 died in a cholera epidemic in the final months of 1850 (two more epidemics followed in 1851 and 1852), and another 30 died in late October, when the *Sagamore* steamer exploded shortly after departing from the city's central wharf.[68] San Francisco's early settlements along the bay also burned down six separate times between December 1849 and June 1851, killing somewhere between 300 and 1,000 residents.[69] City officials quickly realized they needed somewhere—somewhere larger than the city's existing graveyards—to bury the dead.

An 1851 map of San Francisco that was drawn by surveyor William Eddy and shows Yerba Buena Cemetery. At the time, Larkin Street (*far left*) was the western city limit. *William Eddy, courtesy of David Rumsey Historical Map Collection.*

In March 1850, William Eddy, the city's surveyor, staked out a fifteen-acre property on the edge of the city and claimed it was the perfect spot for an official cemetery: it was located along the existing road to the mission, and it was easy to get to. It was also on the very edge of town, surely far enough away from the boomtown by the bay to keep it from bothering any residents. Already, about fifty people had been buried on the site. Perhaps naively, Eddy told the *Daily Alta California* that "there is enough town property in that locality to make a cemetery sufficient to accommodate the dead of the city for the next half century."

Within eight years, Yerba Buena Cemetery was full.

YERBA BUENA CEMETERY

Michael O'Leary of Cork, Ireland, was thirty-two when he died in San Francisco on October 22, 1851. He was buried three days later in grave number 296 in the brand-new Yerba Buena Cemetery bordered by Market, McAllister and Larkin Streets. At the time, Larkin Street was the western city limit.[70] Some newspapers claimed that in its early years, Yerba Buena Cemetery was a beautiful spot with an undulating landscape planted with evergreen oaks and bushes. "The crooked trunk and limbs of their oaks gave a romantic appearance to the cemetery. Under the shade of the trees were handsomely ornamented graves."[71]

Others painted a grimmer picture of the property. The *Annals of San Francisco*, quoted by Helen Marcia Bruner in her 1945 book, *California's Old Burying Grounds*, described the area of Yerba Buena Cemetery as:

> *an unenclosed waste* [that] *lies in a hollow among miserable looking sand-hills, which are scantily covered with stunted trees, worthless shrubs, and tufted weeds. It extends over a large space of ground, and is still among the most dreary and melancholy spots that surround the city. In 1850, there was nothing visible, below and around, but the loose barren sand-hills, with their scattered patches of wild bushes, while above was the boundless, pitiless firmament. The din of the city could not penetrate there. The only sound sometimes heard was the mournful requiem of the distant waters of the bay, when stirred to solemn music by a gale.*[72]

Some of the earliest bodies laid to rest in Yerba Buena Cemetery were transplanted from the North Beach Cemetery. The remains of about eight hundred people were uprooted from North Beach and placed in "'a deep pit, eighty feet in length and twenty-five feet in width located in a dismal spot....Piled up one above the other, or side by side, sleep soldiers and sailors, mechanics and merchants, lawyers and legislators, men of all creeds and professions, from every country and from every clime,' that was not marked by a fence or grave marker," according to Kari Hervey-Lentz.

Within the next few years, thousands more joined them. Estimates on how many people were buried at Yerba Buena vary widely. In 1866, the *Daily Alta California* estimated that the site took in 7,000 to 9,000 dead.[73] A burial register compiled by the Daughters of the American Revolution in the 1930s enumerates about 4,800, not including the North Beach reburials.[74] Significantly, that number also excludes the hundreds or thousands of Chinese dead buried there. The cemetery housed a Potter's Field for indigent dead, as well as Protestants, immigrants and bodies supposedly relocated from Russian Hill and the Sailor's Burying Ground.

Between 1850 and 1860, Chinese newcomers filtered into San Francisco; by 1860, more than three thousand Chinese folks had moved into the city, largely living in the brand-new Chinatown neighborhood.[75] Yerba Buena became their primary burial ground, too, though their graves were separated from the rest by a small incline or hill. One newspaper noted that the Chinese "erected a strange looking place, for the performance of the ceremonial obsequies, peculiar to the genius and custom of their Pagan faith."[76]

As with most of San Francisco's cemeteries, politics played a hand in how Yerba Buena was treated and maintained. In June 1850, perhaps informed by how badly the North Beach Cemetery deteriorated without a barrier protecting it from the outside world, San Francisco mayor John Geary recommended building a fence around Yerba Buena and hiring a sexton to take care of the property.[77] But two years later, the fencing work hadn't even begun. In September 1852, Henry Meiggs, who had helped relocate burials from the North Beach Cemetery and was now a city alderman, offered an ordinance to improve Yerba Buena, build a fence around it and set aside $3,000 for the fence's construction. The council of aldermen adopted the ordinance, which appears to mean that it was sent to an appropriations committee, "where perhaps it may remain for a long time to come," the *Alta* lamented in October 1852.[78]

The *Alta* urged the city to act quickly:

> *If there is any one thing that indicates the intelligence and refinement of a people, it is the respect they have for the dead. The last sad duty that we*

owe to our departed brethren is to see them decently interred, and their last resting place protected from improper intrusion. The many hundreds whose bones now sit in our public cemetery are at all times subject to sacrilegious intrusion. There is no enclosure around this sacred ground, beasts roam all through it, wagons and carriages drive in every direction, and it is as unprotected as any of our thoroughfares.

As San Francisco expanded westward, a lack of fencing was the least of the cemetery's problems. In November 1853, a man was caught in Yerba Buena Cemetery stealing a body from one of the graves. A police officer discovered the crime in progress and shot at the man, but the thief ran away and was able to escape.[79] Although it's impossible to know for sure why this man was helping himself to a corpse, this was a period during which medical researchers would often take bodies from graveyards in order to study them, because medical cadavers weren't yet readily available.

Others were discovered harvesting remains in Yerba Buena Cemetery because decomposition produces chemical compounds that are key soapmaking ingredients, according to an 1853 article in *Chambers' Edinburg Journal*.[80]

Owing to the spongy, springy nature of the soil in the burying-ground of San Francisco, many of the corpses there interred, instead of decaying, have been converted into a substance well known to chemists by the name of adipocere—a substance analogous to, and intermediate between, stearine and spermaceti. In passing the ground this morning to my place of employment, I saw a person busily engaged in collecting the adipocere from exposed bodies. Struck by the singularity of his employment, I interrogated him as to its object, when he cooly replied, that he was gathering it to make soap!

Despite William Eddy's assurances, and for a variety of reasons, the land near Market and Larkin Streets turned out to be a terrible location for a cemetery. The ground was composed of mostly sand, and the high winds in that part of the city often blew the sandy topsoil away, exposing coffins and human remains.[81] At the same time, San Francisco continued to expand, and the land that was once so far away from settled areas was now surrounded by housing and commerce. Larkin Street was no longer the wild, distant boundary of the city; Divisadero Street, more than a mile west of Larkin Street, now had that distinction. In December 1853, less than four years after Eddy had staked out the boundaries of Yerba Buena Cemetery, the San Francisco Board of Supervisors was already looking for a new place to establish a municipal burial ground.[82] Michael O'Leary had been laid to rest only three years earlier, and now his body—and thousands of others—faced the imminent possibility of being dug up and shuttled elsewhere. The *Alta* reported:

> *When the original burial ground was established, on Powell street, it was supposed to be sufficiently distant from the centre of the city, and its founders never imagined that its occupants would ever be disturbed. Now a trace of it scarcely remains, and the still later established cemetery of Yerba Buena, is becoming closely pressed upon by our rapidly growing city. Indeed it is not in a proper location. In a few years, at most, the growth of San Francisco will require that streets shall run through the cemetery ground.*

The newspaper urged city officials to pick a spot "at the farthest verge of the city" or even "beyond the city limits." Leaders, perhaps holding on to hope (despite the fates of San Francisco's cemeteries so far), kept choosing sites within San Francisco for decades to come. In fact, the same night they vowed to find new land for a cemetery, they authorized the Committee on Land Claims to see whether the city could acquire the title to Lone Mountain, which was privately owned at the time.[83]

Burials at Yerba Buena Cemetery ceased in the late 1850s, but the dead there remained in place until 1868.[84] The city raised about $10,000 to move the bodies elsewhere, but the *Alta* reported that that wasn't nearly enough money for the job, and the city had seriously underestimated how many people were buried in Yerba Buena. "Many of these graves are unmarked by stones, head boards, or even mounds," the newspaper reported. "The relatives and friends of hundreds buried here have no knowledge of the exact spot where the deceased lie, and can never learn to a certainty whether they will ever be disinterred, even though the entire yard is dug over. It is proposed that as the work of laying out and improving the tract progresses, the bodies exhumed be collected and at once removed to Lone Mountain."

The city announced plans to disinter the dead at Yerba Buena in 1862 and asked friends and relatives to relocate their loved ones before the city began mass removals. "The removal work was performed by hand labor and much guesswork," Hervey-Lentz writes. "As one journalist noted during a visit to the cemetery, it was hard for the grave diggers to find burials because almost 'all traces of the graves are obliterated. Not even a clew [*sic*] remains by which a row of bodies may be discovered.'"

The city built a temporary vault for remains as they were uncovered. If diggers could identify the deceased, those bones were kept in separate boxes so they could be claimed. Otherwise, they were "dried in the sun to prevent an offensive odor, cast into the common receptacle of the general vault," according to Hervey-Lentz. A reporter from the *Weekly Butte Record*, who visited in 1868:

> *describes the vault in ghoulish terms. About five hundred human skulls were ranked on one side of the vault, many of them with plentiful locks of hair still on them....On the other side of the vault were piled many boxes and old rotten coffins, containing human remains; these were labeled with the names, so as to be reclaimed by their friends....At the farther end of the vault there was a large pile of human remains in all stages of decomposition, thrown together indiscriminately.*

Some of the dead went to the cemeteries on Lone Mountain, while a few hundred were reinterred in City Cemetery, which opened for burials in 1870 near Land's End. But it's anyone's guess how many remained in the heart of the city as Yerba Buena Cemetery was built over. As road and construction

San Francisco City Hall at Larkin and McAllister Streets on the Yerba Buena Cemetery site after the 1906 earthquake. *Detroit Publishing Company photograph collection, Library of Congress.*

projects changed the shape of the Civic Center area after 1870, workers found human remains again and again.

In 1889, a crew, while breaking ground for a new city hall at Larkin and McAllister Streets, found at least seventy graves, including those of many Chinese immigrants.[85] Even then, it sounds like the bodies might not have been moved. Archaeologist Stuart Guedon told the *San Francisco Chronicle* in 2001, "They actually built city hall right on top of these bodies."[86]

One of the graves belonged to Thomas W. Ludlow, a twenty-two-year-old from New York who died of cholera in San Francisco in late November 1850. He was buried in Yerba Buena grave number 730. When crews found his body, almost thirty years later, they became convinced that Ludlow's remains gave them cholera. (This is not scientifically possible—you would need extensive contact with a freshly deceased body, such as washing and preparing it for burial, to contract enough cholera vibrios to get sick.[87]) The following is a report from the *Daily Alta California*:

CHOLERA IN A COFFIN.

Laborers Made Sick by Opening an Old Grave at the New City Hall

Daily Alta California, March 9, 1889

Public attention has again been attracted in a startling manner to the numerous graves that were neglected when the old cemetery on the site of the new city hall was removed over twenty years ago. Among the many coffins unearthed and removed by workmen engaged in excavating for the McAllister-street wings of the city hall, was that containing the remains of Thomas W. Ludlow, a young pioneer who died in November 1850. This coffin was found last Tuesday in a walled grave, surmounted by a handsome headstone, upon which was this inscription:

In memory of
THOMAS W. LUDLOW,
who departed this life
November, 1850.
Requiescat in Pace.
Short, dear husband, was thy race,
Long and painful was thy day; From thy wife so early torn
In life's joy and blooming hoar.

It now transpires that when the coffin was opened several persons who happened to be standing around were taken more or less violently sick. The old files of the Alta *showed that Ludlow died on November 25, 1850, from cholera. At that time the disease was epidemic in this city, and on that day nine new cases were discovered. When it was learned that Ludlow had died of cholera, the people who had been made sick around his coffin by the effluvia from it became badly scared. This scare was considerably increased yesterday morning when the news reached the Health Office that William Curry, a laborer who assisted in opening the coffin, was ill, and physicians had pronounced his sickness cholera. Health Officer Barger visited Curry but found no alarming symptoms in his case. Every possible precaution will now be taken by the Health Department to have the remains quickly and safely disposed of. Dr. Barger states that it would have been much better if the remains had been buried in a loose box, as it then would have exposed the body and all infection would have been killed by the influence of acids in the soil.*

But this incident in 1889 wasn't the end of it. The new city hall at Larkin and McAllister Streets was destroyed in the 1906 earthquake. In April 1908, workmen who were building the city's Main Library on the same site found twenty-five more graves. They stored the remains in a box to be picked up by the coroner's office, but someone stole the skulls before the coroner could fetch them. "It is presumed that they were taken by medical students, or ghouls," the *Chronicle* reported.[88]

The newspaper included an interesting detail that might explain why so many graves were missed before: they were located twelve to twenty-five feet below ground level, much deeper than diggers would have expected. Today, California's health and safety codes only require there to be eighteen inches between the top of someone's casket and the level ground above—two feet if the remains aren't enclosed in something. But those regulations were adopted relatively recently. Back in the 1850s, folks could bury their dead at pretty much any depth they wanted. It's not clear how some of these graves wound up under twenty-five feet of earth.

The spectacle of digging up remains to make room for the Main Library drew people from all over the city, who wanted a glimpse of what lies beyond the grave. "When it became known that the workmen were excavating on the site of the famous Yerba Buena Cemetery, a great crowd collected to watch the uncovering of the graves. Many rotted coffins were discovered, but in every case, the bodies had completely decomposed, owing to the damp and sandy nature of the soil, and only a pile of bones remained to tell that a human being had once been interred there," the *Chronicle* reported.[89]

That's when Michael O'Leary's tombstone was discovered, kicking off a spat between the United Irish Societies and the Society of California Pioneers, each of which believed it had the right to claim O'Leary's headstone almost sixty years after his death. The stone read, "Sacred to the Memory of Michael O'Leary, late of the City of Cork, Ireland, Who Departed this Life October 22, 1851, Aged 32 Years. Requiescat in Pace." R.C. O'Connor and T.P. O'Dowd, representing the Irish Societies, turned up at the excavation site and tried to take the headstone away, but the workers refused to hand it over. Unfortunately, it's unclear what ultimately became of O'Leary's tombstone or his remains.

More burials emerged in 1932 when, as work got underway for the construction of a new federal building at Hyde and McAllister Streets, crews uncovered the marble grave marker for John Connelly, who died on May 5, 1851, at the age of thirty-eight. Connelly was originally from Launceston, Tasmania.[90] According to a report filed with the city on June 8, 1932, at 9:07 a.m. by contractor M.J. Treacy, a worker named Emilio Rigarsio was digging a sewer near the intersection of Leavenworth and McAllister Streets when he found Connolly's bones, along with his grave marker. "It is supposed that there was a cemetery in this vicinity a good many years ago," Treacy wrote. This hallowed ground had been utterly forgotten within decades, and nobody thought to warn the construction teams what they might find once they started digging.

In 1934, as excavations continued, workers found more graves, along with several rare coins. The discovery of skeletons belonging to three graves was reported in the *Chronicle* in March 1934, and H.C. Hall, the civil engineer in charge of the work, said more than twenty graves had been uncovered in the course of construction, some with headstones fifteen feet below the current street level. He added that the remains would not be moved.[91] Presumably, they're still there. The coins included "two $10 gold pieces dated 1843 and 1847. Five Spanish coins of the years 1700, 1733 and 1849 were also found, as well as two of Peruvian money."

Decades later, the graves of ninety-seven early San Franciscans were discovered, beginning in the late 1990s as the city built a new Main Library at Larkin and Grove Streets and transformed the former library building at Larkin and McAllister Streets into the Asian Art Museum. This time, workers were careful to box up the remains and send them to the city morgue, where they were studied, though their identities could not be determined. Ultimately, they were reinterred in the Pioneer Garden at Cypress Lawn Cemetery in Colma, where many other early San Franciscans were ultimately moved.[92]

Rose Pak, a consultant with the Chinese Chamber of Commerce in the late 1990s, urged the museum to hold a prayer ceremony to show respect

The Asian Art Museum, now at Larkin and McAllister Streets on the former Yerba Buena Cemetery site. *Beth Winegarner.*

for the dead and to assuage any concerns among Taoists or Buddhists who might otherwise avoid visiting the museum once it opened. "Basically, you venerate your ancestors," Pak said. "You shouldn't be trampling all over them unless they were interred properly with the right offerings....It's good to appease the spirits of the dead and protect everyone who goes inside the Asian Art Museum."[93]

Museum leaders invited a Tibetan lama to perform a ceremony, designed to protect the site from "misfortune and promote positive healing energies," in October 2001. Another multifaith ceremony took place in March 2003, before the museum opened to the public.[94]

When Yerba Buena Cemetery opened, local newspapers hailed it as a democratic place to bury the dead: "Here lie, side by side, the rich and the poor—no stately obelisk marking the resting-place of the former, but to the living world, reposing as obscure as the latter."[95] Even though dozens of graves have been discovered since the cemetery ceased operations, basic math suggests that many more remain beneath the Civic Center area. And most of those bodies that were left behind after the cemetery closed were those of indigent immigrants, people whose lives are the most likely to be erased and forgotten.

It raises questions about what cities should do when they realize they've built on top of a former burial ground. Should they take the time to excavate,

United Nations Plaza, built on the former Yerba Buena Cemetery, looking toward San Francisco's modern city hall. *Beth Winegarner.*

locate all the remains they possibly can, identify them to the best of their abilities and give them a proper reburial somewhere else? Doing so would mean destroying many civic buildings, including the Asian Art Museum, Main Library, the 50 United Nations Plaza federal building and UN Plaza. Should the city leave them in the ground and go back to recognizing these areas as sacred spaces for remembering and honoring the dead? That might mean abandoning all these buildings and public spaces. Or can civic buildings and sacred spaces occupy the same grounds peacefully?

Today, tens of thousands of people pass through the Yerba Buena Cemetery site every day, shopping at the farmer's market, dropping into city hall or hanging out on the plaza, a popular spot particularly for the city's unhoused population. Hundreds of thousands of people visit the Asian Art Museum each year, and about one hundred thousand drop in to the Main Library on a monthly basis.[96] How many of these people know there's a burial ground beneath their feet? These places honor different types of history and learning, but at the same time, they obscure the history of the land they're sitting on.

Even if nobody knows the names and life stories of the people still buried here, it feels wrong to leave them in obscurity.

Green Oak Cemetery

Yerba Buena wasn't the only graveyard in this part of San Francisco. A lesser-known plot called the Green Oak Cemetery was located essentially across the street. Green Oak was bounded by Market, Mission, Seventh and Eighth Streets and was established in 1849 or 1850. In January 1850, an *Alta* reporter described the three-acre property as "very pretty" and "covered with evergreen oak."[97] An advertisement in the same issue promised that "besides the usual ornaments there will be placed at each corner of the cemetery a cenotaphic tower, to be used upon extraordinary occasions, as the death of a president, governor, or other distinguished man." Folks or churches interested in burial plots were encouraged to contact Charles W. Cornell, the undertaker and agent for the cemetery. Unfortunately, it's unclear how many were buried here and where they might have been moved—if they were moved at all.[98]

5

HOME OF PEACE

SAN FRANCISCO'S FIRST JEWISH CEMETERIES

San Francisco saw six devastating fires between December 1849 and June 1851, killing somewhere between three hundred and one thousand locals and displacing many more. One of these people was Joseph Tobias Bach, who perished in the last of those fires on June 22, 1851. Bach was part owner of a company called Bach, Burnett and Co., which was housed in a brick building on Jackson Street. He burned to death while trying to save the company's storeroom.[99]

The blaze broke out a little before 11:00 a.m. that June morning in a frame house on Pacific Street near Powell Street, and summer winds quickly spread the flames across sixteen blocks of the city between Powell, Sansome and Clay Streets and Broadway.[100] The blaze destroyed two thousand buildings, including the Jenny Lind Theater (which, at that time, housed San Francisco City Hall), the Old Adobe Custom House and businessman and journalist Samuel Brannan's home. One warehouse was saved when workers poured eighty thousand gallons of vinegar on the flames.

The blaze was blamed on the "Sydney Ducks," a band of Australian ex-cons who had a reputation for beating and robbing people and also setting fires and then looting stores during the ensuing mayhem. San Francisco's first Vigilance Committee, founded by none other than Brannan, went after the Ducks and hanged four of them. The rest fled the city for several years.[101]

Bach's remains were badly burned, but he was identified thanks to a spinal condition he had. He regularly wore a plaster brace to support his back, and

A sketch of downtown San Francisco after the June 1851 fire. *Historic American Buildings Survey, Library of Congress.*

parts of the distinctive brace were found with his remains. "The misery he must have endured can scarcely be imagined," a *Daily Alta California* reporter wrote on June 30, 1851.[102]

Emanuel Hart Hebrew Cemetery

Bach was born in New York in 1814 and was laid to rest one week after the fire on June 29, 1851, in San Francisco's first Jewish cemetery. He was a popular man; three hundred to four hundred of his friends and family members came out for his funeral, which was hosted in a shop at the corner of Clay and Montgomery Streets. The procession went with him on foot to the Emanuel Hart Hebrew Cemetery, sometimes called Navai Shalome, bordered by Green, Gough and Franklin Streets and Broadway—a distance of about a mile and a half. "The funeral was attended by a large number of Masons in regalia, and many of Mr. Bach's Jewish brethren. The procession…moved out to the Jewish burial ground on the road to the Presidio, where the remains were deposited with the impressive ceremonies of the Masonic order, and the rites of the Jewish church," the *Daily Alta California* reported.[103]

Established in 1849 by the Temple Emanu-El, the Hart Cemetery served as a burial ground for Jewish residents of San Francisco, as well as Jews from Sacramento, Stockton, Marysville and other parts of California.[104] By the time Bach was buried at the Hart Cemetery, about twelve to fifteen other graves dotted the property. In 1860, an *Alta* reporter described the cemetery as being "fenced in with wooden pickets and quite secluded from the world." Although the site was "far removed from the profane trend of a busy city," the reporter commented that, like in other parts of the city, the sandy soil ultimately made it a poor burial ground. It was subject to high winds, and "the slight covering was not unfrequently blown away and the coffins exposed."

By 1860, the Hart Cemetery was almost full, with room for just about twenty more burials.[105] Temple Emanu-El purchased a block of land just south of Mission Dolores in 1860, and Sherith Israel purchased the adjacent block in 1861.[106]

Today, the two hilly blocks that once housed the Emanuel Hart Hebrew Cemetery are home to dozens of classic San Francisco–style Victorian and Queen Anne houses, with their ornate woodwork and rounded bay windows, and several apartment buildings in a variety of historic and modern styles. Sherman Elementary School, a public K-5 school founded in 1892, is located right across Green Street from where Bach and others were buried. There's no sign of the Jewish graves that once rested here, and there's no way to know for sure if they were all removed once the cemetery was closed. One record shows that about three hundred graves were relocated to the new mission grounds (Bach's was among them), but no one knows whether that was all of them.

Navai Shalome (New) Cemetery and Giboth Olam Cemetery

These new Jewish cemeteries sprawled across eleven acres of open land on property that would eventually become Dolores Park. It's hard to imagine now, but at the time, these lands were considered south of the city limits.[107] They were dedicated in 1860 by Rabbi Julius Eckman, a former spiritual leader at Congregation Emanu-El and the founder of the *Weekly Gleaner* newspaper. It sounds like it was a pretty grand affair.[108]

The audience, which was very numerous, gathered about the platform, on the northern side of the "house for the dead," which is within the enclosure, when Dr. Eckman opened the ceremonies with a dedicatory prayer, after which Mr. Seligman, on behalf of the Emanu-El Congregation, delivered the sacred keys to Mr. Tichner, the President of the Supervisors of the Burial Ground, making at the same time appropriate remarks.

He was followed by Mr. Helbing, President of the Eureka Benevolent Society, who at the same time delivered to the President of the Supervisors of the Grounds, the keys hitherto entrusted to him, when he made some brief

Two Jewish cemeteries were established on the land now occupied by Dolores Park. *Lawrence & Houseworth (publisher), Library of Congress.*

and eloquent remarks. As the keys were tendered to Mr. Tichner, Chairman of the Directors, he responded, ending with the hope that he would be called upon to open the gates to the "House of Rest" (Navai Shalome) no oftener than the Merciful Father deemed best for the good of his children. At half past eleven, Dr. Elcan Kohn, Minister of the congregation Emanu-El, commenced his sermon in the German language. It was eloquent and impressive, occupying about half an hour. After the prayer, the ceremonies closed, and the assemblage returned to town.

The Cemetery is pleasantly located on a side hill, a few minutes walk from the depot of the railroad....It is substantially fenced in, and has a handsome gateway structure. One of its rooms is dedicated to the purification of the corpse, and is arranged to have hot and cold water admitted for that purpose. The whole place, both as regards the grounds and the building, evinces good taste. A better site could not have been selected for the purpose.[109]

These cemeteries took in about three hundred burials each between 1860 and the tail end of the 1800s, when San Francisco's relentless expansion caught up to this part of the city. In 1897, the Mission Park Association organized an effort to improve the entire mission neighborhood, which, by that time, was the most populated area of San Francisco—but one often overlooked by city officials. The association proposed a park "of international quality," possibly with a zoo of some kind, and began eyeing the Jewish cemeteries as a possible site.[110]

As with many efforts to "improve" San Francisco over the years, there was opposition, "with popular sentiment deeming such a park unnecessary, an undue burden to taxpayers, and a scam to fill the pockets of greedy real estate developers; Golden Gate Park [which opened in 1870] already served the city's needs. Mayor James Phelan also opposed calls for investing in a Mission park," Kevin Montgomery wrote for *Uptown Almanac* in 2011.[111] Unwilling to give up, the association launched a new campaign in 1903, and this time, it was much more successful. Voters widely approved a bond measure to purchase the property, and the city took over the burial grounds in February 1905, while burials in the Jewish cemeteries began moving to two new sites in Colma.

Joseph Tobias Bach's grave and headstone (*center*) were moved multiple times before landing in the Hills of Eternity Cemetery in Colma, California. *Beth Winegarner.*

Bach's remains were moved for a second time; his current resting place is in the Hills of Eternity (Giboth Olam) Cemetery in Colma.[112] The monument on his grave bears a lengthy inscription in tribute to his tragic story:

A cruel death thus to abuse thy pow'r
To seize thy prey before its weary hour
To pluck the rose while in its fullest bloom
The sun yet bright thou caused to set in gloom

Death
Reproach me not, I did what was my right
Transplant the tree its fruit I did not blight
I felled not all within the realms of bliss
He flourisheth. Eternal life is his

Joseph is no more
Thy death untimely, brother dear we mourn
Who in thy manhood's prime was from us torn
Thy last dread hour thy faithfulness attests
Thy love sorrows enshrined within our breasts

Verily Joseph Liveth
To thee on earth not many joys were given
For man finds its best reward in heaven
There is thy harvest home, thy blessed abode
With those pure souls who love and serve our God

Sacred to the memory of a man worthy and greatly beloved, God fearing
Charitable and upright

Joseph Tobias Bach

who perished in the 37th year of his age, a victim to the great conflagration
of this city on Sunday the 22nd day of Sivon 5611 AM
corresponding with the 22nd day of June 1851.

His remains were interred here
on Sunday the 29th following.

His soul reposeth in Paradise.

Considering its age, Bach's five-foot-tall gravestone is in remarkably good shape, with just a few cracks on its rear side. At the peak of the monument, the stonemason carved a weeping oak, along with the words אַלּוֹן בָּכוּת, which translate to "weeping oak," referring to the biblical spot where Rebekah's lifelong friend and nurse, Deborah, was buried.

By the spring of 1895, about half of the Jewish cemeteries' graves had moved to Colma, and a year later, only one grave site remained. It belonged to Augusta R. Neustadt, who died in 1875, and her two husbands, James Michael, who died in 1865, and Isaac S. Josephi, who died in 1870.[113] "A tall stone shaft rose above the three tombstones, making it a prominent fixture in the otherwise abandoned landscape and a source of frustration for would-be real estate developers. As long as this grave site remained, the property could not be sold and the land could not be developed," the *San Francisco Call* reported in July 1896.

It looks like the graves were eventually moved, because the trio are now buried in Cypress Lawn Cemetery in Colma, and San Francisco began planning the new city park in the early 1900s. Ideas included a garden, a swimming pool, a miniature lake, a "magnificent stone stairway" leading down from Twentieth and Church Streets, an outdoor gymnasium, tennis courts, a bowling green and a variety of broad-leafed plants, palm trees and an "avenue of trees."[114] Transforming a piece of city property in this way was very unusual, according to a report on the neighborhood's history. "During much of the nineteenth century, cemeteries functioned as parks and open space for urban residents. Often the only large landscaped spaces in a city, cemeteries were used for strolling, picnicking and contemplation. San Francisco is unusual in utilizing a former cemetery to create one of the city's largest parks in the Mission Dolores neighborhood."[115]

However, dreams of a new city park were delayed by the 1906 earthquake and fires. After they struck, the land vacated by the Jewish Cemeteries served as a refugee camp. Like many other city parks, it was filled with small shacks where locals could live until they got on their feet again. The camp operated until October 22, 1907.[116] After that, the city was—rightly—busy rebuilding, but park plans soon resumed. In 1908, workers laid a new system of water pipes beneath the property, spread loam and fertilizer, planted some trees and shrubs and removed the last remnants of the refugee camp, except for the first earthquake shack, Crowley Cottage. It was named for the Reverend Denis Oliver Crowley, the vice-chairman of the Mission Relief Committee and president of the Youth's Directory, and served as "a temporary home for friendless and abused boys between the ages of 7 and 14 years."[117] Crowley

Cottage remained as a reminder of the disaster until about 1960, when it was ultimately removed.[118] Crews paved the streets around the property, created the planted medians along Dolores Street and planted palm trees along the boulevard. In 1913 and 1914, the city added storage and toilets to the property as it slowly became a park, and it built tennis courts in 1913. The children's playground arrived in 1916, replacing a wading pool. The J-Church streetcar line, which runs along the northern edge of the park, opened to the public on August 11, 1917.

Dolores Park has since become a destination for locals who want to play tennis, throw a frisbee for their dog, picnic and drink or relax in the sunshine (this neighborhood is one of the sunniest in San Francisco). It has also hosted many of the city's protests and unique celebrations, including the annual Dyke March, part of Pride festivities, and the Easter Hunky Jesus competition put on by the Sisters of Perpetual Indulgence. It's undergone only subtle changes since the 1910s, including a $7.9 million renovation in 2011. That means there hasn't been a lot of digging—nor have there been many opportunities to find out if anyone's grave still lies beneath these grassy hills.

"There are rumors that not everyone buried in the park was dug up and moved to Colma, and the Advisory Council on Historic Preservation has very strict guidelines on dealing with building sites that also happen to be burial sites," *Mission Local* reporter Heather Smith wrote in 2011.[119] Maybe Augusta Neustadt and her husbands weren't the last to go after all.

Even the city has noted the possibility: "Because the presence of human remains and funerary objects gives a historic property special importance as a burial site or cemetery, federal agencies need to consider fully the values associated with such sites. When working with human remains, the federal agency should maintain an appropriate deference for the dead and the funerary objects associated with them, and demonstrate respect for the customs and beliefs of those who may be descended from them," states the Advisory Council on Historic Preservation's policy statement regarding burial sites.

The Jewish cemeteries at today's Dolores Park were San Francisco's first real attempt at a park-like cemetery, where locals could stroll and picnic among the gravestones, but it wouldn't be the last. Soon, the city began planning something much larger.

6

THE RURAL CEMETERY MOVEMENT ARRIVES

LONE MOUNTAIN AND LAUREL HILL CEMETERIES

J ohn Orr was born in Ireland in 1824, but tracing his life story prior to his arrival in San Francisco in 1850 is tricky, especially since his name isn't uncommon. In 1840, a sixteen-year-old musician named John Orr from Donegal, Ireland, joined the ranks of the U.S. Military in New York. If this is our John Orr, he was a slight lad; five foot, three inches tall, with gray eyes, light hair and a fair complexion. He next appears in the *Daily Alta California* on December 12, 1850, among a list of passengers arriving in San Francisco on the steamship *New Orleans* from Panama.[120] He pops up in a brief newspaper item from January 29, 1852, after he was fined five dollars for fighting with a man named Caleb Cokely, and again a couple weeks later, when he was found in contempt of court.[121] "John Orr was arrested for not appearing at Court to prosecute a suit in which he was the complainant." (Maybe he was suing Cokeley over the fight, but it doesn't say.) But "he was excused on account of sickness," the *Daily Alta Calfornia* reported.

On June 9, 1854, Orr died of unknown causes—perhaps from the same illness that caused him to miss his court date—and was buried on June 10, when he became the first person interred in San Francisco's brand-new cemetery, Lone Mountain. His tombstone read, "In memory of the first inhabitant of this Silent City."[122] John Orr's wife (though it's not clear whether this is the wife of the same John) gave birth to a daughter on September 7, 1854, in Jackass Gulch, deep in the gold country of Amador County.

Lone Mountain Cemetery as viewed from Calvary Cemetery in 1866. *Lawrence & Houseworth (publisher), Library of Congress.*

Lone Mountain Cemetery

The gold rush and San Francisco's population boom forced San Francisco to expand its cemeteries. City officials, realizing they were quickly running out of space in Yerba Buena Cemetery, decided in late 1853 to approach the owner of Lone Mountain's lands to ask whether they would sell to the city.[123] It must have gone well, because by the end of the month, crews were already at work, clearing undergrowth and laying out eight miles of avenues that would run through the cemetery grounds.[124] The footprint of the Lone Mountain Cemetery complex would now be roughly bounded by California, Arguello and Fulton Streets and Presidio Avenue (which, back then, was known as Cemetery Avenue). After witnessing how the Jewish cemeteries at today's Dolores Park became destination spots for strolling and picnicking, and watching as other cities developed similar "garden" or "rural cemeteries," San Francisco leaders wanted Lone Mountain to be part of the trend.

"Some very beautiful spots are brought to view by these improvements, and this season of the year, when the grass and foliage are green and the wild lilac is in bloom and the laurel in berry, is the most favorable time to visit these beautiful grounds," an *Alta* reporter wrote the day before Christmas 1853. They continued:

> Persons living in the city who never go beyond our built up streets have no idea that there is so much of rural beauty as may be found in many little spots within the cemetery tracts. When completed there will be forty miles of avenue traversing the entire ground with a carriage road winding up the sides till it reaches the top of Lone Mountain....We have seen a design of the main entrance on Bush street, which is to be a highly ornamented arch sixty five feet in height surmounted with a figure of the Recording Angel. On the sides of the main entrance are to be four other entrances. The owners of the Cemetery tract have secured the two blocks from the entrance on Bush street in order to prevent any rum shops or buildings of an improper character being erected there.

Orr's grave became part of the massive 170-acre property that sprawled across the middle of San Francisco in an area that now includes Laurel Heights, Anza Vista and the Inner Richmond. It was eventually subdivided into several smaller cemeteries, a "silent city" that would ultimately house more than 136,000 "inhabitants." They were outnumbered by the living by a ratio of only about three to one.

Lone Mountain Cemetery was dedicated on May 31, 1854, in what the *Alta* deemed an "the most pleasing and interesting public ceremony that we have ever witnessed in California."[125] "The weather was exceedingly pleasant, the roads leading to the consecrated ground were in fine condition, and everything conspired to entice the lovers of rural beauty and elevated sentiment to participate in the solemnities of the day. Large numbers of citizens—nearly one half of whom were ladies—were in attendance at the *Dell*—the most beautiful and sequestered spot in the grounds," an *Alta* reporter wrote.

The ceremony included a full choir singing an ode written for the occasion by F.B. Austin. Little is known about the composer, who wrote about the "Greenwood Dell, where near 'Lone Mountain' silent stands a Guardian Sentinel." Local journalist and poet Frank Soule read a long poem, blessing the new cemetery, followed by a dedication from Reverend William Ingraham Kip, who headed San Francisco's Episcopal churches.

"We dedicate this place to the total memory of the departed. We dedicate it as the spot around which in coming years the warm affections of multitudes shall gather, when perhaps they themselves are far away, because here their treasures have been left. We dedicate it as the last resting place of countless generations who are to come after us, until every grass sod is heaving with the buried dead," Kip told the gathered crowd.

As with San Francisco's earlier cemeteries, it's understandable that city leaders thought this one would last a long time. Its pastoral design made it a destination for people who wanted to escape from city life for an afternoon, even if they weren't paying respects to a loved one. Despite its reputation as a "destination" cemetery, burial plots were fairly affordable: a single grave started at five dollars, and a family plot started at fifteen cents per foot in 1867.[126]

At first, though, getting to Lone Mountain from San Francisco's downtown was not easy. "The present mode of access to the cemetery is by a circuitous route, nearly four miles in length, by way of Pacific street [now Pacific Avenue] and the presidio."[127] Opening such a massive new cemetery forced the city to make improvements. "When the western extension of Bush street is graded and planked, which is proposed to be done during the summer of 1854, the distance from the plaza [Portsmouth Square] to the magnificent gateway of the cemetery, about to be erected at the termination of that extension, will be about two miles."[128] In the latter half of 1854, Bush Street opened from downtown to the gates of the cemetery, and Lone Mountain opened a main entrance right where Bush Street met Cemetery Avenue.

By 1862, eight years after the cemetery opened, seven thousand people had been buried at Lone Mountain, with about seventy-five new interments each month.[129] Sections were laid out for the Protestant Orphan Asylum, firefighters, the Typographical Union and many other organizations. Its owners continued to be optimistic about its longevity. "The present proprietors of the Cemetery are J.H. Atkinson, C.C. Butler, and Nathaniel Gray. They think there is room in the Cemetery to bury all of the dead of San Francisco for half a century to come," reported the *Daily Alta California*.

Not everyone felt so positively about the cemetery—or its name at least. Some felt that calling it Lone Mountain was creepy and grim (this was long before J.R.R. Tolkien released his book *The Hobbit*, featuring a Lonely Mountain inhabited by a greedy dragon named Smaug). Even before the cemetery was dedicated, the *Daily Alta California* ran a letter to the editor, complaining about the name:

LONE MOUNTAIN CEMETERY.

DAILY ALTA CALIFORNIA, MAY 10, 1854

A more unfortunate selection of a name for the new cemetery could not have been made than that of Lone Mountain. How lugubrious! How chilling! One's very soul shrinks from it. The idea of desolation, of complete isolation; a mountain in a wilderness; a place of resort for the owls and the bats, and perhaps a solitary wolf—are the thoughts that present themselves to the imagination; a place to be avoided rather than sought after as a final resting place. The idea of the grave is of itself revolting to our nature, and requires no accessories to add to its gloom. What more painful, after having consigned the remains of a dear friend to its embrace, than the thoughts that obtrude themselves into our minds in the silent hours of the night! The "cold grave"—the "clods of the valley"—"the sleep that knows no waking," &c, are all gloomy enough without having that grave in a lone mountain. That is carrying the funeral into all time, and making it perpetual. It partakes too much of the undertaker for my taste. I would not bury the remains of a dear friend in a spot, however beautiful it might be, the name of which conveys the view of utter abandonment, and Lone Mountain does.

We hope that the trustees of the cemetery will give a more cheerful title to their fine grounds. Let it be "Pyramid Mount," "Sunny Side Cemetery," "Mount Olivet Cemetery"—anything rather than Lone Mountain.

—Old Mortality.[130]

LAUREL HILL CEMETERY

That writer got their wish in 1867, when a portion of the Lone Mountain complex became known as Laurel Hill Cemetery.[131] It was inspired by and named after a similar garden cemetery, which was landscaped with plants, trees, statuary and walkable avenues in Philadelphia. The new Laurel Hill Cemetery comprised fifty-five acres, bounded roughly by California, Arguello and Presidio Streets and Geary Boulevard.[132] Around the same time, nearby portions of the Lone Mountain property were divided into cemeteries for Masons, Odd Fellows, Catholics and Chinese, Greek and Russian people.

After the change, Laurel Hill remained a very popular place to bury the dead; ultimately, about thirty-five thousand people were interred on the property, including a small section for Japanese burials, as Kari Hervey-Lentz, an archaeologist who works in the city's Planning Department,

Laurel Hill Cemetery. *Roy D. Graves, Roy D. Graves Pictorial Collection, Wikimedia Commons, public domain.*

discovered recently.[133] While looking through newspaper articles on Laurel Hill, Hervey-Lentz came across a photograph showing an obelisk with Japanese characters near a few rows of small headstones. A copy of the photograph kept in the San Francisco Public Library is labeled "Japanese plot and memorial obelisk to Japanese pioneers at Laurel Hill Cemetery."[134]

The first graves in this 2,600-square-foot section belonged to the sailors of the *Kanrin Maru*, a Japanese warship that docked in San Francisco. Their graves are dated 1860 and include such names as Gennosuky, Tomizo and Minekichi. Kinjiro Inaba and Jisaburo Ban, sailors aboard the Japanese warship *Chikuba* were also buried here. All told, more than one hundred Japanese graves rested in this spot, now within the footprint of a house at 561 Spruce Street. Many were later moved to a group grave in the Nihonjin Community Cemetery in Colma.[135]

Until the mid-1880s, Laurel Hill Cemetery remained a largely rural, open place, where gravediggers were occasionally bothered by wild bears.[136]

THE BEAR AGAIN.

Still Uncaptured, and Holding the Fort In a Graveyard.

Daily Alta California, May 19, 1884

The big black bear which swam from Marin county to the Presidio last Saturday afternoon, and after surrounding the entire United States Army there stationed, wandered off to the Cliff House, is still at large.

Yesterday at 5 a.m., two grave-diggers were at work in Laurel Hill Cemetery, preparing a hole for the reception of a dead Chinese fish peddler, when the bear appeared on the bluff just back of the cemetery and peered into the pit. The grave-diggers howled, and the bear fled to an adjacent quarry, where he took a drink of water and then wandered off into the brush.

The Superintendent of the cemetery applied to the Chief of Police for a force of expert marksmen to suppress the bear, but Counsellor Clark could find no warrant in law for the use of the "finest" for this purpose, and the police were not sent. Philo Jacoby and Dr. Bauer, the two great bearslayers of the city, will have to arrange a hunt with their dogs before the brute is taken into camp, and the outlying hills made safe as promenades for small children. Those who have seen the brute say he is about 400 pounds' weight, and anything but a pleasant customer to meet.

Despite predictions that Lone Mountain would remain an ideal burial ground for decades to come, by the 1890s, it was surrounded by thousands of residents, and dozens of businesses serving those residents' needs. Soon enough, cemetery neighbors began demanding ways to get downtown and back quickly. They rallied the city to extend Sutter Street—which ran through the southeastern corner of Laurel Hill Cemetery—into the Richmond District. They also began gathering support for an even bigger proposition: getting rid of the cemeteries entirely.

Just the idea of extending Sutter Street through the cemetery kicked off an epic fight among residents, particularly between property owners who wanted the road and wealthy San Franciscans who had purchased large plots in the cemetery or whose loved ones might be dug up or paved over in the effort.[137] Henry Sonntag, a trustee of Laurel Hill Cemetery, noted that the proposed extension of Sutter Street would disrupt an area in the burial ground known as Senators' Row, which included the tombs of U.S. senators James Graham Fair, Aaron Sargent, William Gwin and David Broderick.

Broderick died in September 1859, after a duel with David Terry, the former chief justice of the California Supreme Court. The former allies

Left: U.S. senator David Broderick in 1855. He died in 1859 in a duel with California Supreme Court justice David S. Terry and was buried in Laurel Hill Cemetery. *Brady-Handy photograph collection, Library of Congress, Prints and Photographs Division.*

Right: California Supreme Court justice David S. Terry. *Wikimedia Commons.*

had, in recent years, developed an intense political rivalry, starting when Terry lost reelection to the California Supreme Court that same summer. He blamed Broderick, who had launched an antislavery campaign that opposed Terry's faction. Indeed, one of Broderick's last statements before he succumbed to his gunshot wounds was, "They have killed me because I was opposed to slavery and a corrupt administration."[138]

Even if the senators hadn't been buried there, the area proposed for the Sutter Street cut wasn't ideal. It was quite steep and would require extensive grading work that Sonntag argued would "virtually destroy the whole cemetery." Going through with the plan would be "needless desecration," he said.

Others claimed that "no important graves" were in the path of the proposed extension aside from Broderick's. One local proposed that "this large monument of the dead statesman need not be moved, as it would stand exactly in the middle of the street, which could, if desired, be widened at that point. The honored tomb would be a splendid ornament for the thoroughfare, standing as it does on the crest of the hill."[139]

The fight over Sutter Street became moot in late 1896, when a local attorney, W.A. Lawson, discovered a California law barring the construction of roads through most cemeteries, Laurel Hill included.[140] The law dated to 1859, when the state legislature authorized the incorporation of cemetery associations. Within the law was a section that read, "No street, road, avenue or thoroughfare shall be laid through such cemetery." The Laurel Hill Cemetery Association had been incorporated in 1867, after the law took effect, which meant Sutter Street couldn't be extended through the burial grounds. Today, maps of San Francisco show that Sutter Street was never extended; it stops at Presidio Avenue, formerly Cemetery Avenue, at the eastern border of what was once Laurel Hill Cemetery.

The movement to close and move the cemeteries was much more successful than the effort to extend Sutter Street, even if it took a while. In 1890, Richmond district residents fought against a proposed crematorium that was to be built near the corner of California and Laurel Streets at the northern edge of the Laurel Hill Cemetery. Two locals argued before the city's Health and Police Committee in August 1890 that "the neighborhood is now laboring to have the cemetery removed and does not want to be saddled with a still greater evil." No one spoke on behalf of the cemetery or proposed crematorium, so the committee sided with neighbors and voted against it.

Beyond the "evils" of cremation, locals also worried about the health risks associated with living near a cemetery. Just as San Francisco was coming into its own as a city, the germ theory of disease was beginning to take hold in Europe. The idea that illnesses were caused by something too small to see had actually been around since ancient Judea, but few people trusted it. Instead, most believed that diseases, including syphilis, cholera and the bubonic plague, were caused by either personal failings or miasmas—bad air, particularly air that came from corpses. In many ways, it made sense: such odors smell awful and might even make people queasy, just like many illnesses do. Humans' primitive disgust reflex keeps them away from these smells; it's an instinct that keeps them alive. And it's true that many diseases spread through the air—just not in the way people once believed.

French scientist Louis Pasteur gets most of the credit for developing germ theory, though there were others, including British physician John Snow (not the one from *Game of Thrones*) and Italian entomologist Agostino Bassi, who described similar ideas earlier in the nineteenth century, and Persian physician Ibn Sina, who proposed a kind of contagion theory in 1025. Pasteur experimented extensively with the relationship between microorganisms and disease in the 1860s, including trials that involved fermentation and the practice of boiling liquid to kill germs—pasteurization—that would later be named for him. By the 1880s, germ theory was beginning to overtake miasma theory in most people's minds and cemented itself after viruses were discovered in the 1890s.[141]

It's not clear exactly when germ theory made its way to San Francisco, but between the 1860s and the end of the nineteenth century, germ and miasma theories seemed to battle each other in the minds of San Franciscans, especially when it came to the massive cemeteries that took over the Lone Mountain area.

In early 1868, a brief item ran on the front page of the *Daily Alta California*, calling for deeper graves to be dug on Lone Mountain and predicting that soon, the cemeteries would need to be moved entirely. Among other things, the clergyman was afraid that corpses unearthed by strong winds could pose a threat to public health.[142]

HOW WE BURY OUR DEAD.

Daily Alta California, February 5, 1868

We do not remember that the subject of the following communication from a well known clergyman has, as yet, been agitated in this community, but it is one which will soon be of much importance to San Francisco, and it can do no harm to have the matter inquired into, to see if the writer's fears are well grounded. Lone Mountain and Calvary Cemeteries are so situated that they must soon be surrounded by the residences of our citizens, and the question raised by our correspondent will be one of vital interest to the public:

Editors Alta: I feel constrained to ask you to call public attention to an evil which I have long noticed, with no little pain. It has fallen to in mournful duty to bury the dead in ten or twelve different cemeteries, and nowhere have I seen graves so shallow as in "Lone Mountain," and nowhere have I known deep graves so necessary as there. The ground is sandy and liable to be removed by our violent winds in summer—and the wind blowing over the Cemetery must spread whatever miasma may exist there over the city—hence the paramount importance of very deep graves. I know not whether any law exists prescribing the legitimate depth of graves. Perhaps my fears may be groundless, but I do fear that many of the dead there interred will at a future day have to be reinterred. Is it not absolutely certain that the exhalations from those shallow graves of the thousands there buried will, sooner or later, affect the health of the city?

—Clericus.

On July 20, 1895, the city's Health and Police Committee heard a petition from the Richmond Improvement Club to prevent San Francisco's cemeteries from selling any more burial lots.[143] At the hearing, club president Charles Hubbs argued that maintaining a cemetery "in the heart of a city was a menace to the public health." This is where we begin to see the combination of miasma and germ theories take hold locally, particularly as an argument for removing San Francisco cemeteries. Ultimately, the committee denied the petition, saying they didn't want to take action until "an expression of opinion was given by the people," meaning a citywide vote.

But leaders in the Richmond District didn't give up. In October 1895, Hubbs insisted, "The Richmond people, to a unit, earnestly desire the removal of the five big graveyards in the hills above their abodes" and that the city's board of health could close the cemeteries any time it wanted to "for sanitary reasons."[144] The *San Francisco Call* published comments from a doctor, William Mays, who described the condition of the Lone Mountain cemeteries in gruesome (and scientifically bogus) terms:

The bodies under the sand discharge the gasses of decay easily up in the open air. On damp foggy times when the atmosphere is heavy, the odors from these exhalations are very apparent. In winter the rain water seeps into the sandy soil of the graveyards and finally is drained into the low ungraded places in the many vacant lots of the district. There these noxious waters stagnate, becoming all the more poisonous. For a long time a pool stood at the corner of First avenue and Point Lobos road, opposite the schoolhouse, which had its source in the cemetery. It was a most unhealthy spot, and several deaths occurred in the near vicinity. The place was finally sewered and drained.

The *Call* seemed to concur:

All civilized nations bury their dead outside the city limits, conceding that the emanations from putrefying bodies exert an injurious influence upon health. For it is admitted that these polluted emanations not only breed specific disease, but they aggravate sickness and generally increase the rate of mortality. The products of the decomposition of graveyards may be classed as distinct organisms or ferments (low forms of cell life) and the deadly mephitic gasses. These, after impregnating the soil, emerge through it and infiltrate the lower strata of atmospheric air, and are thus wafted along streets and into dwellings. The putrefactive gasses possess great expansive energy, forcing their way through the densest wall, and often rending asunder airtight coffins.

Professor Selmi of Mantua has published an interesting account of the poisonous organisms he discovered in the stratum of air hanging over a certain cemetery. San Francisco is peculiarly unfortunate as regards the cemeteries, situated as they are in elevated positions, with the greater part of the City lying below and to windward of them. Nine-tenths of the year trade winds blow directly over the cemeteries into the City. To make the danger still greater our fogs and mists, always unhealthy, follow the same course, and taking up the exhaled poisons in passage descends upon the City with tenfold virulence. Yet it is a matter of common remark among medical men that outbreaks of diphtheria and other filth diseases are constantly occurring near the cemeteries, in dwellings and streets where the drainage and sewerage are as perfect as art can make them. Where burying grounds have existed or still exist in cities, it has been abundantly proved that their neighborhoods are unhealthy and that epidemics of those diseases which arise from blood poisoning are proven to be there manifested in enhanced virulence.[145]

Along with all this, Richmond residents feared that the presence of so many burials was tainting San Francisco's underground water supply. The *Call* claimed that earth and stone were "excellent" purifiers of water and that the porous nature of San Francisco's soil made it an ideal place to establish surface wells for drinking water. However, it simultaneously argued that sinking any such wells was "out of the question in any part of the city near to and lower than the cemeteries."[146]

Richmond residents' battle began to pay off in January 1896, when Mayor Adolph Sutro barred the city's cemeteries from selling any more lots for future burials. Sutro's order cut the cemeteries off from any new sources of revenue—and revenue was the only way the grounds were kept in good condition. It was a literal death knell: graveyards began to fall into disrepair, making neighbors even more eager to evict them. Sutro's order also required cemeteries to move somewhere outside of San Francisco city limits.[147] But it didn't take effect quite yet. Many expected that the cemetery associations would take the city to court over the move. In the meantime, San Francisco's graveyards continued to operate for a few more years.

The San Francisco Board of Supervisors looked at the issue again in January 1900. At the time, the *Call* noted that previous boards had considered the question of closing the cemeteries, "but for one reason or another no action has been taken upon it." The newspaper used strong language in support of ousting the dead and, in doing so, made it clear that civic progress was more important than respect for the deceased and their families. Burying bodies in "thickly settled urban districts" is "evil," the paper claimed. "In our case, the evil is augmented because the cemeteries within the city stretch as a barrier against the westward extension of municipal growth. They interpose between the main portion of the city and one of its finest and most attractive residence districts."[148] San Francisco ultimately succeeded in passing a ban on burials in 1900, scheduled to take effect on August 1, 1901. The cemeteries continued to welcome the dead until that date, and some challenged the law by continuing after the deadline.

Even though cemeteries like Laurel Hill were closed to new interments, they didn't relocate right away. Many continued to fight the city's law, and in the meantime, they became forlorn, neglected places amid one of San Francisco's largest neighborhoods. The 1906 earthquake devastated the already shabby graveyards, splitting statues and toppling headstones.

San Francisco's burial grounds became prone to theft and mischief.[149] "Coffins were taken from mausoleums and bones strewn about. Entire skeletons were carried away to be used as Halloween decorations or, despite their apparent protestations, presented to high school and college biology and anatomy teachers….Children hiking the cemeteries became accustomed to discovering gruesome relics such as bones protruding from the ground. Some actually engaged in kickball contests with human skulls," Michael Svanevik and Shirley Burgess wrote. "On foggy nights college fraternities found the desecrated cemeteries a made-to-order venue for macabre initiation rites, drinking bouts, and sexual orgies. Anguished neighbors complained of hideous laughing and eerie screams emanating from the darkened graveyards."[150]

By the late 1880s, new cemeteries began to open in Colma, a tiny, unincorporated town just south of San Francisco. San Francisco's Mission Street now extended all the way through Colma, making it easy for folks to travel there by horse and carriage. Streetcars also ran to Colma, including special funeral streetcars that could carry coffins and mourners to the new cemeteries. Once burials were banned in San Francisco, Colma cemeteries became the closest place for San Franciscans to bury their dead. And in the early twentieth century, when San Francisco leaders formally sent eviction notices to the city's settler dead, entire cemeteries began moving south.

The Lone Mountain cemeteries finally admitted it was time to go and began relocating to Colma in the 1920s. Laurel Hill was the last to relocate, beginning its move in 1940. Cemetery workers erected screens so that passersby couldn't see what was happening, and remains were packed into redwood boxes of various sizes, along with any keepsakes that had been buried with the dead.[151] The cemetery tried to locate next of kin for the dead buried there, but only about one thousand graves were moved by private parties. Cemetery leaders removed more than thirty thousand bodies from the Laurel Hill grounds, but the start of World War II delayed their reburial. Tens of thousands were held in a kind of limbo in temporary storage until the war effort settled down. Many weren't reinterred until 1948.[152]

Even when officials thought they'd finished unearthing the dead, they rechecked the Laurel Hill grounds and found 189 more graves. Some sources say an additional 3,000 were still unaccounted for. Many of the marble and granite grave markers were broken up and used in other city projects, including the construction of the Wave Organ and the breakwater at Aquatic Park. Once the work was finished, the Laurel Hill property was sold to offset the costs of moving all the graves. Removing the graves cost an estimated $121,544, while reburial cost more than $200,000.[153]

Today, the area that once belonged to the Laurel Hill Cemetery is now the Laurel Heights neighborhood, which is mostly residential, dotted with low-slung apartment buildings and single-family homes. A strip of shops along California Street offer coffee, groceries and other goods. Fireman's Fund bought a large chunk of the former cemetery property in 1953, which later became the home of the University of California, San Francisco's Laurel Heights campus, hosting some medical and administrative offices.[154] But the property is getting ready for another transformation: as of mid-2021, developers were planning to build 752 new apartments, along with shops and other amenities. As of 2023, that hasn't happened yet.

For a while, the University of San Francisco, Laurel Heights, campus bore a plaque acknowledging that the property once belonged to the dead and is registered as a California Historic Landmark. The bronze marker read: "Former site of Laurel Hill Cemetery, 1854–1946. The builders of the west, civic and military leaders, jurists, inventors, artists and eleven United States senators were buried here—the most revered of San Francisco's hills." Unfortunately, the plaque was removed, possibly stolen, sometime before January 2012.[155] It has not been replaced.

Diane Barclay, a spokeswoman for the California Office of Historic Preservation, said it's not unusual for plaques like this one to go missing, victims of theft or vandalism.[156] But these plaques are often funded and purchased by the people or organizations that first nominated them for

The site of Laurel Hill Cemetery is a California Historical Landmark, but the commemorative plaque disappeared sometime before 2012. *Beth Winegarner.*

landmark status and are only replaced if someone from the public wants to pay for them.

Lone Mountain, too, has transformed from the days when it gave its name to a family of cemeteries. Although the dead were never buried on its peak, for decades, a tall white cross on top of Lone Mountain looked out over the cemeteries on its flanks. In the 1930s, it became home to the San Francisco College for Women. The college changed its name to Lone Mountain College in 1969 and was acquired by the University of San Francisco in 1978. Today, it's a beautiful and steep campus generously planted with grass, shrubs and large, fragrant lavender bushes. Cypress trees shade portions of the mountain as paths wind among the gardens, in much the same way they once did in Lone Mountain Cemetery. A tall, ornate archway stands just above Lone Mountain's entrance on Turk Street, echoing the gate that once welcomed mourners as they entered the graveyard from Bush Street.

Laurel Hill was the first cemetery to welcome the dead to Lone Mountain, but it wasn't the last. Soon after Laurel Hill became a separate graveyard, this part of San Francisco was home to six burial grounds.

7

THE "BIG SIX"

LONE MOUNTAIN'S CEMETERY SUBDIVISIONS

L one Mountain was originally set up as one large, 170-acre burial ground, but it wasn't long before civic and religious organizations began dividing the land into separate cemeteries for their respective members. Although city historians often refer to this complex of graveyards as the "Big Four," including Laurel Hill, Masonic, Odd Fellows and Calvary Cemeteries, in reality, there were at least six, including the Chinese Cemetery and the Greco-Russian Cemetery, both established in this area as it became San Francisco's "silent city." One of the only remaining signs of this massive cluster of burial grounds is the San Francisco Columbarium, a mausoleum that was once part of the Odd Fellows Cemetery.

Lone Mountain's graveyards were established in a time when so-called rural or garden cemeteries were becoming popular across the Western world. Not only did garden cemeteries push the sad business of death to the periphery of city life, but they were also landscaped and decorated much like parks, making them ideal destinations for a picnic or a stroll through nature. It might seem bizarre that residents would want to relax on a stone bench among memorials to the dead—particularly when they didn't want to live next door to a graveyard for fear of illness and miasma—but humans are wonderfully contradictory creatures.

Unfortunately, these beautifully planted and appointed cemeteries were not available to everyone. Although there's evidence that many working-class San Franciscans joined fraternal organizations like the Masons and Odd Fellows so someone would take care of their burial and funerary needs

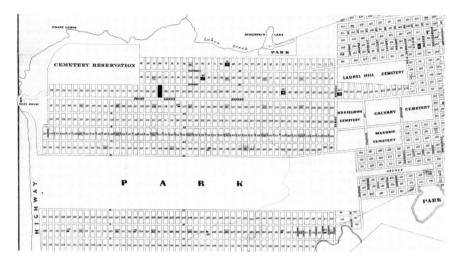

Detail from an 1868 map of the city showing the "big four" cemeteries (*right*) and City Cemetery (*upper left*). *San Francisco Board of Supervisors, courtesy of the David Rumsey Historical Map Collection.*

when they died, the truly poor and many immigrants could not be buried in these spaces. Indigent residents who died penniless were buried at the city's expense in Yerba Buena Cemetery or, later, City Cemetery.

It's not clear how much it cost to be buried in the Masons or Odd Fellows Cemeteries; in advertisements, the Masons only claimed their plots went for "moderate prices," and the Odd Fellows didn't advertise.[157] It was almost certainly more than the cost of burial in San Francisco's municipal cemeteries. In Calvary Cemetery, plots cost $0.60 per foot. Burying an infant cost about $10 (about $250 today, adjusted for inflation), while burying an adult cost around $15.[158] The class divide endures, even after death.

At the same time, organizations that established these idyllic garden cemeteries found it difficult to keep them looking fresh and vibrant. In many cases, individual plots were private, and it was up to the family of the deceased to pull weeds and trim shrubs around their loved one's grave. Many families chose not to do this, and plenty of people who came to San Francisco in search of gold had no local family to look after their remains once they died. Meanwhile, the cemetery associations and fraternal organizations hadn't established endowments and other forms of long-term income that could pay for groundskeepers and staff; that idea was still decades away. As a result, cemeteries that started off as grassy, green parks soon looked shabby and unkempt. Their decline became part of the reason residents in an ever-expanding San Francisco wanted the cemeteries to move out.

Lone Mountain's "Bix Six" cemeteries were meant to finally show San Francisco's dead the respect they were due. But just like before, the stories of these burial grounds show how city leaders' lack of foresight doomed these graves almost as soon as they were put in the ground.

ODD FELLOWS CEMETERY

Edith Howard Cook was six weeks shy of her third birthday when she died on October 13, 1876, from merasmus, a severe form of malnourishment often caused by another illness. Her parents, Horatio Nelson Cook and Edith Scooffy Cook, buried her in Odd Fellows Cemetery in a casket made of lead and bronze with a small glass window that revealed her face and torso. Edith had long blond hair and was buried wearing a long white dress and holding a single red rose. Her hair and dress were decorated with lavender, and eucalyptus leaves were laid beside her.[159]

The Odd Fellows Cemetery was located on the western slope of Lone Mountain, bounded by today's Geary Boulevard, Turk Street, Arguello Boulevard and Parker Avenue. Before it was Geary Boulevard, it was the Point Lobos Toll Road, which opened in the early 1860s and ran from the corner of Kearny and Clay Streets all the way to the Cliff House near

Odd Fellows Cemetery as viewed from the cemetery office or main water tower sometime between 1879 and 1891. *Wikimedia Commons, public domain.*

Point Lobos at the western edge of the city. At the time, locals who wanted to trek out to Lone Mountain to stroll the grounds or to bury their dead would have had to pay a $0.50 toll (about $9.50 today) to get there.[160] As an aside, Point Lobos did not get its name from wolves (*lobo* is Spanish for "wolf") but from sea lions, which Spanish explorers called *lobos marinos*, or "sea wolves."[161]

It's not clear when the Odd Fellows established its cemetery on Lone Mountain. Some put the date in 1854 or 1860. But the *Daily Alta California* reported in July 1853 that the Odd Fellows bought the thirty-acre property more than two years earlier, placing the date, most likely, sometime in 1851. Although the Odd Fellows had already buried a few members there, the newspaper reported that a collection of squatters had "forcibly seized" the land, requiring the Odd Fellows to "oust the sacrilegious wretches from the sacred resting place of the dead."[162]

The Odd Fellows did not formally dedicate the cemetery until November 27, 1865. "The day was heavenly—one of those gloriously beautiful which peculiarly mark the incoming of the vernal season subsequent to a rain," the *Daily Alta California* reported. The burial ground featured a large concourse and a natural amphitheater created by the shape of the hillside.[163]

Within a few years, however, the cemetery was in trouble. In 1870, the California legislature approved a request from the Odd Fellows to borrow money to pay its mortgage on the property.[164] It was out of debt again by 1875, but in 1893, the Odd Fellows proposed deeding the property to the City of San Francisco, along with $100,000, in the hope of preserving the burial ground in perpetuity.[165] "As each individual plat-owner has an absolute right to the property he purchased, the association has not the power to divert the land from its present purpose, and it, therefore, must remain as the city may see fit to condemn it. It is for the purpose of preventing this latter alternative and to secure for the plat-owners a perpetuation of their rights that the association is making the present move."[166]

That didn't happen, and by 1899, the cemetery had fallen into serious disrepair. One day, seven-year-old Willie Elsie, who lived near the cemetery, was playing with another boy, digging for gold, when they dug up human bones, coffin fragments, pieces of a burial shroud and a pair of boots. These finds were taken to the morgue, but neither an autopsy nor an inquest was expected to follow.[167]

At least twenty-six thousand people were buried in the Odd Fellows grounds between the cemetery's opening and 1901, when burials ceased. Even so, Odd Fellows superintendent George R. Fletcher was arrested for burying a deceased man, Earl Charles Printero, on August 31, 1901, well after the August 1 deadline.[168] Fletcher was later released on bail.

When it came time to move San Francisco's cemeteries to Colma, the Odd Fellows did not take as much care as some of their counterparts. They advertised in an effort to find next of kin for the remains but didn't get many responses. As they began to disinter the bodies, workers sometimes held up sheets of canvas to keep passersby from being able to see the work, but other times, the process took place in plain view. "An army of diggers was hired to locate bodies. Stories persist that remains were often uncovered in full states of preservation," Michael Svanevik and Shirley Burgett wrote.[169] Passersby could not only see but also smell the process. "It was not 'pretty,'" wrote city planner William Proctor in a 1950 analysis. "The smell of death was often present, even though the remains had been laid to rest from 30 to 70 years previously."[170]

About twenty-six thousand sets of remains were moved, ostensibly, to Greenlawn Cemetery in Colma. But Greenlawn buried them in a separate parcel, which is divided from the main cemetery grounds by a Best Buy store. Today, the mass grave sits within a vacant lot on Colma Boulevard, between a Best Buy and Home Depot Pro. The lot is fenced off, and the burial site is marked with a single monument to the Odd Fellows who rest there. Descendants of the Odd Fellows dead cannot visit their loved ones' graves.

It's hard to know just how many of the Odd Fellows dead were left behind, but people who live in the former cemetery's footprint occasionally find them. In 2011, while homeowner Erika Karner was renovating her property, workers unearthed a casket containing the remains of a two-year-old girl.[171] A year later, volunteer researchers, including Alex Ryder, were able to identify the girl as Edith Howard Cook by re-creating a plot map of the old Odd Fellows Cemetery and discovering that her family plot was beneath Karner's home. As they researched Cook's possible identity and history, her body was temporarily reinterred in Colma under the name Miranda Eve. She was permanently reinterred in June 2017 at Greenlawn Cemetery.

Cook's body wasn't the only one left behind when the cemetery moved. The remains of at least three other people have been discovered in the area that once belonged to the Odd Fellows Cemetery, according to volunteer investigator Elissa Davey.[172]

Before discovering Cook's casket under their garage floor, Karner says her family occasionally heard ghostly children's footsteps around their house. Those sounds stopped once the girl's body was found and reburied. "I'm not sure where I stand on where the soul goes, but my hope is…if she was still hanging around here figuring out where she needs to be, that her being identified will give her a little peace and she'll potentially go off and be with her family, where she needs to be," Karner said. "We felt that if anything, she was a friendly spirit. If she wants to stay and play, we're totally OK with that!"[173]

The San Francisco Columbarium

The San Francisco Columbarium, built in 1898 at the northern edge of the Odd Fellows Cemetery, was the first structure of its kind on the West Coast. With room for 8,500 niches to hold cremated remains and memorabilia, the columbarium functions as a large, shared mausoleum where remains may still be interred today—at least for those who have reserved their spaces. When plans for the columbarium were first drawn up in 1895, leaders expected there might be room for ten thousand niches.[174]

"The building proper will be of brick and cement, and the interior finishings of a plain yet attractive character. It is proposed to commence work within the next thirty days, in order that it may be finished before the rainy season. The building complete will cost $40,000," cemetery superintendent George R. Fletcher said in August 1895. This was ambitious; San Francisco's rainy season usually begins in November or December.

And then, just a few years after the columbarium opened for business, San Francisco voted to end burials and other interments within city limits and eventually ordered all the cemeteries to move south. When the Odd Fellows Cemetery began its relocation to Colma in the 1930s, the original plan was to tear the columbarium down. But it was saved from destruction in 1934, when it was declared a memorial under the Homestead Act. Even so, nobody seemed to want it. The building changed hands several times over the years and fell into ruin for more than four decades until the Neptune Society bought and began restoring it in 1980.[175]

When longtime caretaker Emmitt Watson began working at the columbarium in 1987, it was still in terrible shape. "They had mildew, cobwebs. The stained-glass windows were cracked, dirty. There was water in the walls, and it smelled damp. Homeless people used to camp here before the Neptune Society purchased it, and you could still tell," he said.[176]

Today, this space is grander than the Odd Fellows originally envisioned it could be. The central floor is paved with polished inlaid stone in the shape

The Columbarium is a neoclassical resting place for cremated remains that was built by the Odd Fellows fraternal organization in 1865. *Photographs in the Carol M. Highsmith Archive, Library of Congress, Prints and Photographs Division.*

of a compass rose, with its petals pointing to the wind's twelve quarters. Each of the ground-floor rooms is named for a different Greek wind, and the stained-glass windows depict a variety of angels. It was named a San Francisco Designated Landmark in 1998.

Though the San Francisco Columbarium is the most well-known structure of its kind in the city, it isn't the only one. There is a second small columbarium located within Grace Cathedral at California and Taylor Streets. This columbarium was established in 1985 and still has room for new inurnments, according to the cathedral's website.

MASONIC CEMETERY

The Odd Fellows wasn't the only fraternal order to set up burial grounds near Lone Mountain for its members. The Freemasons, who established a San Francisco lodge in 1849 in a building at 728 Montgomery Street in downtown San Francisco, purchased about thirty acres of the Lone Mountain grounds in 1854.[177] Their plot was in an area bounded by today's Turk, Fulton and Parker Streets and Masonic Avenue (the last of which got its name from the cemetery).

One of the dead laid to rest in the Masonic Cemetery was James Reynolds Boyce, who was born in Portsmouth, Virginia, in about 1829. He came to California sometime before 1860, when a census taker found him living in Campo Seco in the heart of gold rush Calaveras County, working as a miner. He was living with a man named John Ryan, a fellow miner who was born in Ireland around 1826.

By 1866, Boyce had moved to San Francisco, where he worked various jobs on the docks—longshoreman, stevedore, porter—while he moved around the city. Sometime before 1880, he moved into the What Cheer house, a men-only house once located at Sacramento and Leidesdorff Streets.[178] The house didn't allow any liquor on the premises and also housed San Francisco's first free library and museum. It may have gotten its name from a friendly greeting common during the gold rush, in which people said, "What cheer, partner?" to each other. The house was destroyed in the 1906 earthquake and fires.

The Masonic Temple Center (*foreground, right*) at Post and Montgomery Streets. *Historic American Buildings Survey, Library of Congress.*

It looks as if Boyce never married or had children. He died on August 4, 1881, from unknown causes at the age of fifty-two. He was buried in the Masonic Cemetery.[179] Between 1854 and 1901, when San Francisco stopped allowing burials, about 19,900 dead joined him.

The Masonic Cemetery property, like the rest of Lone Mountain, was noted for its beauty as well as its views of the ocean and surrounding hills. The cemetery was "laid out with walks, and ornamented with shrubbery and monuments of exquisite taste." At the entrance, probably somewhere along Masonic Avenue, was a porter's lodge with a bell that rang out as funeral processions arrived. To the left of the entrance sat a Pioneer's Plot for early contributors to San Francisco, and in the center of the cemetery stood a fountain that was fed by an artesian well. Cemetery superintendents kept the burial grounds "in splendid order," according to newspaper reports from the era.

"The views of the ocean and coast range of hills from the western acclivity partake of the sublime as well as beautiful. Almost any clear day, and particularly just after a storm, the sound of the breaking waves on the Seal Rocks can be heard with distinctness in any part of the grounds."[180] The Seal Rocks, located just off San Francisco's western shore, are more than a mile from the former Masonic Cemetery.

San Francisco's human residents weren't the only ones to enjoy their time among the headstones on Lone Mountain. Two black swans made their home in Masonic Cemetery in 1880. "A pair of beautiful and perfectly black Australian swans have been received by John S. Gray, Secretary of the Harbor Commissioners. They are of more than average size, and have been presented by him to the Masonic Cemetery Association, to be placed in one of the three fountains in that cemetery."[181] They must have been gorgeous.

In 1887, the Masonic Cemetery's secretary predicted there would be "abundant room for burials for years to come."[182] Nobody knew what was coming—that burials would soon be banned within city limits and the cemeteries would be evicted in the ensuing decades.

Before the Masonic Cemetery could begin its move to Colma, seventeen families whose loved ones were buried in the graveyard went to federal court to block the cemetery's removal. Their suit went all the way to the U.S. Court of Appeals for the Ninth Circuit, but they ultimately lost. The court approved the sale of the property in a 1930 ruling, rejecting the families' argument that ordering the removal of their loved ones' graves violated the families' constitutional rights.[183]

The court noted, "The cemetery in question has been virtually abandoned. Its graves and tombs are neglected. It has been overgrown with rank vegetation. No funds have been provided by the lot holders for its proper maintenance, and there is no likelihood that such funds will be provided." Around 1915, the cemetery's directors "made an appeal to the lot holders for an annual contribution for the maintenance of the cemetery, but the returns following such appeal were not sufficient to cover the cost of postage stamps on letters sent to the lot holders," let alone the cost of cemetery upkeep.

On top of that, the lessons of the devastating 1906 earthquake and fires were still fresh in everyone's minds, including those of the Ninth Circuit judges. The Lone Mountain cemeteries blocked many of San Francisco's major arteries into the Richmond District, where more than 100,000 residents lived by the 1930s, "mostly in wooden houses built very close together." With the cemeteries in the way, firefighters' access was limited, the court noted.

When it came time to relocate the cemetery, Masonic officials reached out to everyone they could find who was related to one of their dead. They were able to match about 50 percent of the interred with living relatives, and only about half of those agreed to pay the costs of moving the graves.[184] Historian Tamara Shelton attributed this to "rapid population turnover" that diminished "the number of people who had a direct relationship with the dead."[185] Families arranged to move about 5,600 of their loved ones to other burial grounds, mostly to Woodlawn Cemetery in Colma. That left roughly 14,300 in the ground. The Masons asked the city to extend the deadline for removals in December 1931 and won an extra thirty days. But the odds remained stacked against them: they sent about 5,000 letters notifying relatives and asking them to get in touch. About 2,500 of them were returned by the post office, which could not find their addresses.[186]

Ultimately, many of the Masonic Cemetery's graves were reinterred in a common plot at Woodlawn, marked with a memorial to the San Francisco pioneers. Their headstones were used in various projects around the city. James Boyce's, now broken into several pieces, lines a drainage ditch in Buena Vista Park, along with many others from Lone Mountain's dead. The paving project was part of the Works Progress Administration's efforts to put people back to work after the Great Depression. Crews working on the ditch were told to place the gravestones face-down out of respect for the dead, but they didn't do a perfect job.[187] Some, like Boyce's, are face-up and readable.

The gravestone for James R. Boyce was repurposed to pave a drainage channel in Buena Vista Park. *Beth Winegarner.*

Untold numbers of graves were left behind. When the University of San Francisco broke ground on its first major building, the Gleeson Library, in 1950 on land that once belonged to the cemetery, workers found at least two hundred bodies after a backhoe uncovered a mausoleum.[188] In 1966, during the construction for the University of San Francisco's (USF) Hayes-Healy residence hall, the crew "came upon so many bones and skulls that they refused to continue working until the human remains were moved from the site," according to Alan Ziajka, USF's official historian. It happened again in 2011, when excavation work began for USF's John Lo Sciavo, S.J. Center for Science and Innovation: workers found fifty-five coffins, twenty-nine skeletons and several skulls.

Given all these finds, it's likely that many more of the Masonic Cemetery's graves remain in the ground, waiting to be rediscovered as construction comes and goes in this part of the city.

Fraternal organizations weren't the only ones to establish cemeteries during Lone Mountain's heyday. Catholic leaders also built a large graveyard here, the first Catholic cemetery in San Francisco since Mission Dolores began burials in the 1770s.

Calvary Cemetery

Calvary Cemetery, which opened in the early 1860s, was the largest cemetery in San Francisco yet. At forty-nine acres, bounded by Geary and Turk Boulevards and Parker and St. Joseph's Avenues, it was many times bigger than the Catholic cemetery at Mission Dolores. The church laid out considerable funds—$50,000 in the 1860s—to hire renowned Bay Area landscape architect William O'Donnell to design the space. It was planted with oaks, laurels, shrubs and ceanothus and featured a variety of pathways that converged in the middle of the cemetery in a large M shape in honor of the Virgin Mary.

Under O'Donnell's guidance, "In the fall [of 1862], shrubbery is to be set out, of a character to withstand the winds."[189] At 421 feet, Lone Mountain isn't the highest peak in the city (that's Mount Davidson at 928 feet). But the

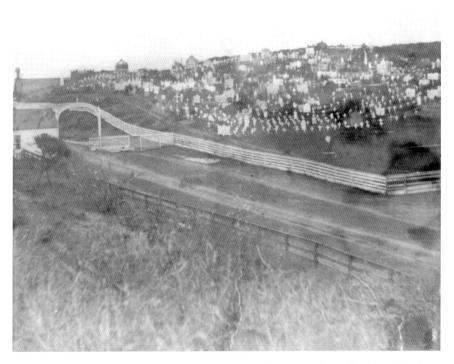

Calvary Cemetery in the 1860s with Point Lobos Toll Road (now Geary Boulevard) in the foreground. *Lawrence & Houseworth (publisher), Library of Congress.*

peak of Lone Mountain, located within the Calvary grounds, "commands one of the finest views....It overlooks the city and bay, beyond Hunters Point, and to the Alameda shores, way up the mouth of the Sacramento, the shores of Marin, the Presidio, Golden Gate, Headlands and the Pacific Ocean."

Calvary was consecrated on a November day in 1860 by Archbishop Joseph Alemany and soon became the primary place for Catholics to be buried in San Francisco.[190] By the time it was relocated in 1940, it held about fifty-five thousand graves.[191] It also became almost a small city unto itself, where people stole grave decorations and bodies from the ground, fought and even died in the bushes, as happened to one poor man in June 1869.[192] He was reportedly heard moaning, "as though he were seriously ill." About two weeks later, his remains were found in the shrubs that had been so meticulously planted by O'Donnell's team. A *Daily Alta California* reporter guessed that the man died of either illness or poisoning.

Even before the cemeteries fell into real disrepair, vandals had their way with them from time to time. In 1887, a man named Felix Ferret (yes, really) was fined fifty dollars for desecrating the graves of his ex-wife's relatives in Calvary Cemetery after their divorce. The former Mrs. Ferret was the one who reported the crimes to the police.[193] The alternative to the fine was spending fifty days in the county jail.

The people of San Francisco always love a story of buried treasure, and in 1897, the *San Francisco Call* gave them one—straight out of Calvary Cemetery.[194]

TRUTH OF THE TREASURE

Large Amount of Money Really Buried in Calvary Cemetery.

Charles Godella Was the Mysterious Mexican Who Started this Sensation.

San Francisco Call, June 17, 1896

The rumor of the burial of a vast amount of money in Calvary Cemetery has at last been traced to its original source. The story goes that one day while Contractor Broderick was overseeing his men widening the sidewalk of Geary street opposite Central avenue, and pulling down the earth of the cemetery, an old Mexican drove by in a cart and told Broderick that there was a vast amount of wealth hidden in the exact locality where the men were excavating.

Rumor had it the next day (Sunday) that two well-dressed men were seen to leave that locality laden with a heavy sack, which they carried between them.

As is usual in a case of this kind the amount of money buried took on fabulous proportions. It was quoted by some to exceed $150,000, while every one in Richmond was positive that there was buried certainly no less than $100,000.

Charles Godella is an old man who has lived out near Calvary Cemetery for years.

"About twenty-eight years ago," said Godella yesterday, "I was sitting in the sun in the old Avenue resort when it was owned by Mike O'Brien. This was then the half-way house for coaches going out to the Cliff. I saw a man standing up on the high ground of the cemetery near the chapel, which then stood near to Geary street. The stranger came down and spoke to me. He had a sandy mustache and looked like a workingman. He asked me if there was any objection to a man digging in the cemetery.

"I told him I thought there was and that he might be arrested for trying to steal bodies. He then asked me if there was any objection to digging in the night. I told him that I thought this would be still worse, because the superintendent slept very near the chapel.

"After this he said: 'My friend, an old partner of mine, is now in the Broadway jail. Two years ago he robbed a bank in San Francisco of $20,000. He kept $2,000 and buried the rest first in Laurel Hill Cemetery, and then fearing that this spot was discovered took up the money and reburied it in Calvary Cemetery, seventy-five feet north from the chapel, near to the headstone that had the name of O'Connor on it.'

"I never saw the man again," said Mr. Godella, "but I myself thought soon after that I would try my luck there. I dug around a gravestone that was partially buried in the sand. As near as I could make out 'O'Connor' was inscribed on the stone. I felt around in the sand with a long crowbar and about six feet down felt a solid mass of some length. This, I am positive, however, was only an old wall that had been sanded over by the wind.

"I gave up the search then, and the story had been almost forgotten by me until a few weeks ago I saw the men digging in the same spot. I told them if they found any treasure there to be sure and give some to me, as I was the only man that knew about it. I am pretty sure that no man has found anything there, but at the same time I believe that what the man told me twenty-eight years ago was the truth."

Contractor Broderick said something yesterday that in part corroborates the story of the peanut vender. "A day or two ago I found about six feet down from the surface," said he, "a small square box made of stones. This was about a foot square, but the top stones had been evidently removed and placed back loosely. So if this was where the treasure was first buried some one evidently dug it up long ago."

Godella said that the money was buried in an iron box surrounded by stones. The question remains now—has the treasure really been unearthed and has Godella been the lucky man? He denies this vehemently. He owns considerable valuable property in Richmond.

In the fall of 1900, a man named Thomas James struck gold of a different kind in Calvary Cemetery: he began living in a vault that belonged to the Hensler family, "surrounded by gruesome coffins, chilly marbles and acres of graves," according to a *San Francisco Call* reporter.[195] James had come to California from Butte, Montana, a year earlier. He'd worked in a dry goods store in Butte but hadn't been able to find work since he arrived in San Francisco. When his money ran out, he landed on a very inexpensive place to call home.

By mid-November 1900, James had been living in the tomb for almost two months and would have continued doing so if he hadn't been arrested. Officials only learned about his creative abode because he hung his laundry out to dry in the cemetery, and a passing police officer noticed it. A *Call* reporter visited James in prison and was able to pry a detailed account out of him regarding how he was able to sustain himself in a house of the dead.

In an article titled "Most Weird Bedroom in San Francisco," this reporter called the Hensler vault "one of the handsomest in the cemetery," but as with many burial sites around the city, it was falling apart, the interior

An illustration of Thomas James cooking in his tomb apartment in Calvary Cemetery, 1900. *From the* San Francisco Call, *November 18, 1900.*

Thomas James, who was arrested for living in a tomb in Calvary Cemetery. *From the* San Francisco Call, *November 18, 1900.*

thick with dust and mold. But James was able to find comfort there, making a bed of burlap and carpeting and decorating the walls with a print of a battle scene in the Philippines and a picture of then-president William McKinley. During the day, he begged on the street for food and stored it in the vault in the funeral urns that once had been used to hold flowers. He made a stove from a five-gallon oil can, used candles for light and played solitaire for entertainment.

At one point, the reporter asked James if he was ever afraid, living among the dead. "Afraid?" he responded. "What of? Those dead people couldn't be any deader than they were, and they were so dead they couldn't budge. Dead people are all right; they're the only kind I ever met that'll let you alone."

San Francisco's cemeteries were about to close to new burials by the time James moved into the Hensler tomb, but it would be another three decades before Calvary Cemetery pulled up stakes and moved to Colma. It was among the last of the city's burial grounds to concede to the city.

Calvary's disinterment process was, reportedly, the most orderly among those on Lone Mountain. The work was screened from public view, and excavations were performed by hand with a priest supervising at all times. Once removed, the remains were taken by hearse to Holy Cross Cemetery in Colma and buried the same day. City records show that 55,000 graves were dug up, and 39,307 went to Holy Cross, while the rest were reinterred in other family crypts, plots or vaults. Holy Cross includes a Calvary Mound marker to let visitors know where those remains were reburied.[196]

Remarkably, when crews performed excavation work in 2017 along Geary Boulevard between Masonic Avenue and Lyon Street, where Calvary used to be, they found plenty of grave markers but no bodies. Holy Cross agreed to take the stones, posting on Facebook, "We received these remnants from the contractor this morning and are busy researching what names we can decipher." Preliminary research indicated that most of the dead whose names were etched on the stones had been relocated to Colma, even if their markers had not.[197]

This brings us to the end of the so-called Big Four. But there were two other cemeteries located near the Laurel Hill, Calvary, Odd Fellows and Masonic Cemeteries on Lone Mountain. It's likely that they're often left out because they belonged to immigrant groups who experienced racism and exclusion in the United States.

Chinese Cemetery

There were few Chinese residents in San Francisco before 1850, but immigrants poured into the city with the gold rush. At first, Chinese communities in San Francisco buried their dead in Yerba Buena Cemetery. After that burial ground closed, Chinese residents built a stonework receiving vault in Lone Mountain Cemetery in the early 1860s. "When important members of the community died, their bodies were brought to the vault and the community held rituals around [it]," writes Kari Hervey-Lentz. Newspapers claimed that the vault held about 150 to 200 sets of remains at a time before the bones were sent home to China.[198]

Rising anti-Chinese racism forced the community to abandon the vault. Chinese immigrants were wrongly blamed for outbreaks of disease, and their cultural practices, including their funeral and burial practices, were viewed by white San Franciscans with deep suspicion. Local bigotry forced Chinese immigrants to keep hunting for new cemetery grounds. For a time, they were allowed a seventeen-acre plot at the western edge of Lone Mountain, bounded by today's Arguello, California, Euclid and Palm Streets. Meanwhile, the beautiful vault, with its stonework arch and sun ray–

A sketch of a Chinese settlement in the suburbs of San Francisco, 1856. *Historic American Buildings Survey, Library of Congress.*

like beams over the doorway, became a storage shed and tool shop for Laurel Hill's groundskeepers.[199]

But soon, Chinese burials were pushed even farther west. "First they were deprived the privilege of interring in Laurel Hill Cemetery; next they were forced to occupy a narrow space near Lone Mountain; and for the third time they were forced to vacate premises to which they are justly entitled," a *Daily Alta California* reporter wrote in 1877.[200] Just as Chinese groups secured the rights to their burial place near Lone Mountain, the San Francisco Board of Supervisors, caving to pressure from neighbors of the Laurel Hill Cemetery, ordered Chinese burials to be moved somewhere else.[201] Ultimately, they were pushed to the very outer reaches of San Francisco at City Cemetery, which opened in 1870.

The last of the Big Six cemeteries near Lone Mountain belongs to San Francisco's early Greek and Russian immigrants.

GRECO-RUSSIAN CEMETERY

The Greco-Russian Cemetery, established on eighteen acres bounded by Golden Gate and Parker Avenues and Turk and North Willard Streets, was dedicated in the 1870s by Bishop Johannes of Russia and overseen by the Greek-Russian-Slavonian Orthodox Eastern Church and Benevolent Society. For several years, it was well maintained and saw sixty or more burials. However, Bishop Johannes returned to Russia in the 1880s, leaving the church leaderless. At the same time, the value of the land surrounding the cemetery was increasing rapidly. Three unidentified members of the Benevolent Society couldn't resist the temptation to cash in. They sold off portions of the cemetery property—without the permission of the church authorities in Russia or the families of those buried on the site.

By 1888, when Bishop Vladimir arrived from Russia to visit the church and tour the cemetery, the property was in ruin. "All that now remains of the once large and beautiful burying ground is a small triangular corner on the edge of a sandy gulch, surrounded on two sides by a miserable rail fence, the third side being entirely unprotected/without gate or barrier of any kind. The place presents a most neglected aspect, the crosses and headstones being knocked sidewise, and the graves—among them that of Very Rev. Paul J. Kedrolivansky, formerly archpriest of the Russian Church in this city—being daily trodden underfoot by cows and other domestic animals."[202]

Bishop Vladimir was "deeply shocked" by the state of the burial ground and told a *Daily Alta California* reporter that, once he established himself in San Francisco, he would have the graves removed from the cemetery and moved to a better spot, and he would sell the property. Presumably, the money would go to the church.[203]

It's not clear what happened after that, but in January 1893, a crew that was working on extending Aldine Street (now a portion of Golden Gate Avenue) unearthed five bodies on the cemetery property. An excerpt from a *San Francisco Call* article tells the story:

EXHUMED BODIES.

A Scraper Unearths Five While at Work.

A Street-Extension Job Which Turned Out to Be More Exciting Than Was Expected.

San Francisco Call, January 30, 1893

James O'Brien had a startling experience on Saturday last. He is a contractor and was hired to grade a street in the city outskirts, which he started in to do on the preceding Monday. All went smoothly until Saturday, when his troubles began. He was using a two-horse scraper when one of the teams, going a little higher than any of the others, caught on something and held for a moment and then moved on again. The driver following the scraper stepped into what he thought was a hole, but on looking down he saw that he was standing in a coffin.

His feelings can better be imagined than described. His fellow workmen assisted him to replace the cover of the box and the work went on.

Later in the day another casket was found, and then three more in a bunch, but this was too much for the constitution of the drivers and they stopped work very willingly when quitting time came. The residents in the neighborhood are very nervous and do not go about much nights just at present, but would have probably overcome their squeamishness had not a boy named Walter Lewis stumbled across a skull in the dark, breaking it. He buried the two pieces in separate places and then went out and spread the story among his acquaintances.

Yesterday quite a number of people visited the place, and, upon searching, found many pieces of human bones, probably the remainder of the poor mortal whose skull had been found the night before. Two of the coffins were lying exposed when a CALL reporter visited the place yesterday afternoon, and although the tops were removed by someone in the crowd no marks were found whereby the corpse could be identified.

If the graves in the Greco-Russian Cemetery near Lone Mountain were eventually relocated, it's likely they moved to City Cemetery, where a new Greco-Russian section was established by 1887.[204]

A Horse Cemetery?

Between 1874 and 1896, a massive horse racing track called the Bay District Racing Track drew crowds to inner Richmond for entertainment and betting. It was bounded by First Avenue (now Arguello Boulevard), D Street (now Fulton Street), Fifth Avenue and Point Lobos Road (now Geary Boulevard) next door to the Lone Mountain cemeteries, particularly the Odd Fellows Cemetery, and just north of Golden Gate Park.[205]

In November 1897, just a few days after Thanksgiving, a San Francisco man, Richard Struther, told the *Call* that he'd seen a spectral horse running the path of the former racetrack as he was heading home after an evening with friends.[206] The newspaper suggested that racehorses were buried on the site.

Struther described the ghostly horse as "wild-eyed and fiery, with tossing mane, floating tail and steaming nostrils." He thought it was a fleshly horse until he saw it run through several fences instead of jumping over them. "Past the old grandstand he rushed at top speed, then gradually slowed down to a walk, stopped, walked back, and, when he reached the grandstand again, disappeared like a flash."

The *Call* reporter quickly connected the vision to "a burial place, but little known"—a horse cemetery within the racetrack grounds.

"What do I imagine it was?" Struther said. "Why, it was the ghost of some horse that was revisiting the scene of its old-time exploits. Maybe it was the anniversary of the animal's death, or maybe it was the anniversary of some famous victory it had won."

The End of the "Big Six"

The fight to end San Francisco's cemeteries was as long as it was messy. Early residents of the Richmond District began agitating for the removal of their sepulchral neighbors by the end of the 1860s, and by 1901, the

San Francisco mayor "Sunny" James Rolph said, "The duty of government is more to the living than to the dead. We must provide for the expansion of our city." *Bain News Service photograph collection, Library of Congress.*

city was convinced to ban any further burials in the cemeteries still operating at that time. During the early part of the twentieth century, then-mayor "Sunny" Jim Rolph proclaimed, "No feeling is more honorable or creditable than respect for the dead." However, he added, "The duty of government is more to the living than to the dead. We must provide for the expansion of our city."[207]

Eventually, the majority of voters agreed with him. In 1937, they overwhelmingly approved a measure forcing the cemeteries to relocate San Francisco's graves elsewhere. The rural cemetery movement, at least in this city, was over. And the "silent city" of the dead at Lone Mountain became a noisy one, a chorus of vehicle engines, horns, industry and human voices. And many of the city's early dead remain beneath their tires, beneath their feet.

What duty does the city have to its dead now? And what duty does it have to the living who might want to know that they live and work on top of graves that were erased and forgotten?

Lone Mountain wasn't even San Francisco's final effort to create a massive and permanent burial ground. But it was one of the last times the city made an effort to remove the dead before wiping the slate clean and building on top of them.

8

LEFT BEHIND

CITY CEMETERY

Thomas Wood, born in Fairfax, Virginia, was twenty-two when he enlisted in the U.S. Military on June 3, 1847, to fight in the Mexican-American War. He reenlisted numerous times until the Board of Medical Survey deemed him too worn out to continue serving. He received his final honorable discharge on November 27, 1881. Wood decided to head to San Francisco, even though he didn't have a home, a job or any friends lined up. After his twenty-five dollars ran out, he poisoned himself.[208]

When Wood's body was found, his pockets contained "a bundle of honorable discharges, nicely tied with red tape, and a number of affectionate letters from a married daughter living near the old home, back in old Virginia."[209]

Wood's body remained at the city morgue as folks with the San Francisco Coroner's Office attempted to arrange an honorable burial, but many cemeteries would not take him, likely because of his death by suicide. Ultimately, he was buried in San Francisco's City Cemetery "with no one by to say even the poor words, 'dust to dust, ashes to ashes!'"[210] Wood's grave was marked with a rusty white plank bearing only a number, 1,116, that was partially buried in drifting sand just off the shores of the Golden Gate.

City Cemetery

City Cemetery was meant to be San Francisco's solution to the problem of Yerba Buena. The old municipal cemetery was full and falling apart. It was now surrounded by the city and located right where leaders wanted to build city hall. The transition was far from seamless. Yerba Buena was at capacity by the mid-1850s, but City Cemetery didn't open until 1868 and didn't see its first burials until 1870. Some of Yerba Buena's dead moved to the cemeteries on Lone Mountain, but thousands more remained in the heart of the city.

Only 267 graves from Yerba Buena were definitively moved to City Cemetery, though there could have been more that weren't documented.[211] And it's entirely possible that some of these graves were on their second move—from North Beach to Yerba Buena and then to City Cemetery. If so, these two hundred acres of remote coastal land, bounded by Thirty-Third and Forty-Eighth Avenues to the east and west, the Pacific Ocean to the north and the Point Lobos Toll Road (now Geary Boulevard) to the south, became the final resting place for them.

The city made some effort to improve the look of the graveyard with plants and shrubs, but there were no trees in and around City Cemetery when it opened, nothing to protect these graves in sandy soil from being buffeted by strong winds off the Pacific Ocean.

Almost from the start, officials at City Cemetery weren't keeping spotless records. Despite the number on the headboard that marked his grave, Wood wasn't the 1,116th person buried in City Cemetery. When a *San Francisco Call* reporter asked the gravedigger how many graves there were, the gravedigger replied, "I numbered up to three thousand, and then began with 'one' again."[212] In February 1882, when the *Call* ran its story on the cemetery and the fate of Thomas Wood, 4,118 people were buried there or possibly more—cemetery workers said they sometimes buried two people in one plot. It was a busy place. By 1882, City Cemetery was burying 40 people a month.

At least eleven thousand of those buried at City Cemetery were indigent, and the city footed the bill to bury many penniless San Franciscans in a Potter's Field here. For the average resident, a grave at City Cemetery cost eight dollars; far less than, for example, the Jewish Cemeteries at Dolores Park, where plots were sold for thirty to forty dollars.[213]

Because City Cemetery basically welcomed everyone, it included dozens of smaller cemeteries. It provided plots for graves moved from the Chinese and Greco-Russian Cemeteries and sections for Jewish, French, German, Italian, Japanese, Scandinavian, Slavonic-Illyric and Black Freemason burials. By 1887, there were nineteen plots associated with local societies and associations and another twenty-six connected to Chinese community groups. Historians believe more than 10,000 Chinese residents were buried in City Cemetery over its years of operation, though only 3,700 or so remain.

Many cultures around the world have beliefs and practices that revere their ancestors, both at home and in the cemetery where loved ones are buried. This is true in Chinese cultures; Qingming, for example, is a day of visiting ancestral graves to sweep them clean and bring offerings of food, tea and spirit money to burn along with fragrant joss sticks. Burial rites were and are also very important to these communities. Historian Wendy Rouse writes:

> *Proper ritual following the death of a* [Chinese] *relative or friend was essential not only to the soul of the departed but also to the happiness, harmony, and well-being of those left behind. Elaborate ceremonies awakened onlookers of both worlds to the tragic event that had occurred. From the moment of death and for generations afterward the deceased were remembered in annual ceremonies performed religiously by their descendants. Thousands of miles of ocean and residence in a strange land modified, but failed to break, the continuity of these traditions.*[214]

During the late 1800s, Chinese in San Francisco largely didn't regard local cemeteries as permanent resting places. Most of the Chinese who came to San Francisco in the years after the gold rush planned to stay only long enough to make good money before returning home again. Chinese community associations took on the responsibility of burying their brethren in San Francisco if they died here and also handled the task of returning their bones to China after a period. Otherwise, if a body was "buried in a strange land, untended by his family, [the] soul would never stop wandering in the darkness of the other world."[215]

Although local Chinese societies built a number of monuments within City Cemetery—one of them, the Kong Chow Temple, remains there to this day—individual graves were generally marked with a simple board or brick painted with an inscription in Chinese.

Shantang (Chinese community) representatives kept track of graves and secured the necessary permits to disinter the bodies, typically a few years

The Kong Chow funerary monument marks the site of Chinese burials in City Cemetery, now Lincoln Park Golf Course. *Beth Winegarner.*

after burial. They paid $10 per disinterment to the city, $2.50 of which went to the cemetery itself. The bones were cleaned if needed and sealed in a tin box marked with the name of the deceased. They were stored in Chinatown before they were sent home to China.

Many western Europeans, including those who settled in San Francisco, didn't understand these customs. Western traditions hadn't placed any importance on connecting with or tending to ancestors for hundreds of years, particularly not once Christianity spread across the world. Those who came to settle and colonize North America left the remains of their forebears behind in European churchyards, possibly to never return. And what they didn't understand, they didn't respect.

Chinese residents of California faced horrific racism, and their cemeteries and burial rites became targets, too. White and European San Franciscans complained about Chinese burial and exhumation practices and often used the "abatement of nuisance" euphemism as an excuse to close San Francisco's cemeteries or limit the activities of Chinese residents.

Other times, white locals didn't bother with euphemisms; their bigotry was stated openly. The Richmond District Improvement Club was thrilled when the city agreed to close City Cemetery in the late 1890s.

In a resolution, the club celebrated "getting rid of this pest-breeding spot and forever remov[ing] from the sight of visitors to the district the pagan rites of scraping the flesh from the bones of deceased Chinese who had been buried there, which to our people was a sickening and dreaded sight, once seen not soon to be forgotten." Meanwhile, vandals who visited City Cemetery often picked up Chinese grave markers to play with, throw at one another or steal.

Reverence for the dead in general at City Cemetery wasn't high on many San Franciscans' list of priorities. Even so, City Cemetery operated in relative peace for the first ten or fifteen years of its existence—that is until a wealthy neighbor moved in and, like many of San Francisco's other rich and powerful, saw dollar signs where others saw sacred ground.

Enter Adolph Sutro

Adolph Sutro was born in Aachen, Prussia, on April 29, 1830, and came to California with the gold rush in 1850.[216] In the 1860s, he developed and

Mayor Adolph Sutro owned land next door to City Cemetery and played a role in halting burials in San Francisco. *Brady-Handy photograph collection, Library of Congress, Prints and Photographs Division.*

built a massive tunnel beneath the mines in Gold Country, meant to eliminate flooding and make the mines safer and more efficient.[217] The tunnel made Sutro very wealthy, and in the 1880s, he returned to San Francisco and began buying up land. One of his purchases was that of a cottage on a bluff overlooking the ocean, now known as Sutro Heights. Another was that of the Cliff House, which he transformed into a "fairy tale Victorian Castle."[218] He turned his estate into an elaborate public garden decorated with statues, gazebos, topiary and much more. And he built the Sutro Baths, an extensive complex of public swimming pools filled with ocean water and heated to different temperatures. All of this was happening right next door to City Cemetery.

Sutro thought the fee to ride the streetcar from downtown San Francisco to his seaside attractions ($0.10; about $3.07 in the 2020s) was too expensive, so he built a sightseeing railroad of his own. Work began on this new railway, or "cable road," in August 1886. As proposed, it would run west from the corner of Geary Street and Cemetery Avenue (now Presidio Avenue), north to California Street, west along California Street to Lake Street and then around the north side of the City Cemetery, ending its journey at the Cliff House. "The Sutro road will be one of the most picturesque in the country. For two miles it will command charming views of the Golden Gate and ocean, and for more than a mile it will run along the bluffs at a height of 125 feet above the level of the sea."[219]

Sutro's design involved building a section of trackway near the intersection of Thirty-Third Avenue and Clement Street—right over a grave plot owned by the Knights of Pythias.[220] Sutro had been negotiating with the Knights of Pythias for a while, and apparently, each side thought they had an agreement. Sutro believed he had permission to build the railway through the cemetery plot once he paid to move twelve bodies buried there. The Knights of Pythias thought Sutro would pay $250 to move each body, while Sutro originally offered $150 a piece. But in later negotiations, Sutro offered $5 to move each of the bodies, and the Knights of Pythias refused.

At this point, Sutro became furious, accused the fraternal organization of trying to blackmail him and said he would build the railroad through the graves "without asking anybody's leave."[221] By the time local judge issued an injunction on the work, Sutro's workers had torn down cemetery fences and laid tracks right on top of several graves. "Considerable tilling" had been done over them, and there was "no attempt made to carry out the original arrangement to move the bodies." The tracks also ran close to the tombstones of other graves.

Sutro's engineers claimed that there were no graves under the railway and that the land in question had been "allowed to fall into decay." He accused the Knights of Pythias again of trying to "scotch the old man for a few dollars." He told the *San Francisco Call*, "The work is done and the restraining order is of no effect. There will be no trouble, as the whole thing is over." A *Call* reporter noted that defacing, breaking or removing tombs was a violation of the penal code, but Sutro wasn't prosecuted for it.

It wasn't Sutro's only run-in with the law. On a late September morning in 1889, two members of San Francisco's Health and Police Committee visited City Cemetery and discovered that Sutro had inexplicably enclosed 160 acres of the cemetery with a fence.[222] He had rented the land for several years for use as a pasture for his animals, but the fence was built without permission, and the board of supervisors ordered him to remove it. A few days later, the city sent a surveyor to establish the correct boundary lines.[223]

Sutro tried to put his own spin on the situation, sending his agent, Alexander Watson, to tell officials that "there are but 200 acres of land in the cemetery, and that if Mr. Sutro had taken up 160 acres only forty would be left, which is absurd," the *Call* summarized. Watson said Sutro had had his land surveyed and was well aware of where the boundaries were, insisting that the city was the confused party. "The charge of the Superintendent of the cemetery that Mr. Sutro has absorbed any of the city's land, Mr. Watson claims, was caused by that official's ignorance of where the lines really run."[224]

Despite his claims that he meant the cemetery no harm, Sutro's actions tell a different story. In February 1891, he invited a number of local and federal dignitaries for a visit. His guests that day included San Francisco mayor George Henry Sanderson, several members of the city's board of supervisors, two park commissioners, U.S. Army major general John Gibbon and Colonel George Mendell, chief of the Engineering Corps of the Division of the Pacific. He wanted to show them a two-hundred-acre area of San Francisco, some of which belonged to City Cemetery, because the military hoped to build defensive fortifications along the San Francisco coastline.

Sutro Heights and seal rocks as viewed from Ocean Beach. Adolph Sutro owned these lands next door to City Cemetery. *Library of Congress, Prints and Photographs Division.*

"The Government is anxious to secure as much of the tract as possible, but will not pay a fancy price. It has been suggested that the Government give the city a part of the Presidio Reservation in exchange for the cemetery tract," the *Daily Alta California* reported.[225]

But that wasn't the only reason Sutro invited everyone out to the cemetery. He urged his guests from the federal government, Mendell in particular, to begin the process of condemning the entire cemetery. Mendell said he had the authority to condemn fifty-five acres of it but wanted to see how San Francisco residents felt before exercising that authority.

"Nearly all present expressed an opinion in regard to the matter, and the general impression seemed to be that it would be to the best interests of the city to permit the Government to condemn the cemetery. Then the city would be rid of an eye-sore, adequate protection would be obtained for the harbor of San Francisco, and with the money the city could purchase a cemetery outside of the city and pay for the removal of the bodies now in the City Cemetery," the *Alta* reported.[226] It's no surprise that Sutro's elite and powerful guests felt this way. None of them represented the indigent, Chinese or other local societies whose people were buried there. They didn't see it as sacred ground, just an "eye-sore."

The same day all those dignitaries visited Sutro, a *San Francisco Examiner* reporter trekked out to the cemetery to describe its current state. The article depicted the sharp divide between those with resources and those without—"Desolate and Forsaken," the headline read. While some areas were evidently well tended, including the Jewish and Chinese sections, others appeared "uncared for and seemingly forgotten," the reporter wrote.

> *Here lie the city's pauper dead. The dry grass tangles thick and long, and here and there are bunches of scraggly brush—skeletons of dead bushes. But there is not a tree in the whole place. Not a slender fir tree, and not a bit of green vine or growing twig. The neglected graves stretch out row after row. At the head of each was once a board numbered with the number of its silent owner. There are no names upon these headboards, and wind and weather have worked hard to obliterate even this simple mark of identity. Many of the numbers are illegible.*[227]

It was written as if to support Sutro's proposal to condemn the cemetery. And once Sutro had Mendell's commitment, he didn't waste any time. By mid-February 1891, he was before the board of directors of the Real Estate Exchange, telling them that the U.S. government should condemn City

Cemetery and pay the city for the fifty-five acres needed to build harbor defenses; he suggested the rest of the land should be turned into a city park.[228]

That's essentially what happened. The U.S. government bought fifty-four acres in 1891 and turned them into Fort Miley, a coastal fortification that included a battery for rifled guns and another for twelve-inch mortars, as well as barracks and other buildings.[229] Sutro became San Francisco's mayor in 1895, and in January 1896, he signed an order barring San Francisco's cemeteries, including City Cemetery, from selling any more lots for future burials. Property owners in the Richmond District—the same ones who were behind efforts to oust the cemeteries on Lone Mountain—helped get the ordinance introduced and passed.

It was the beginning of the end for San Francisco's burial grounds. The move blocked local cemeteries from earning revenues, and the *San Francisco Call* predicted that the cemetery associations would sue.[230] They did.

Cemetery associations argued that the ordinance didn't do anything to prevent burials, since there was room for eighty thousand more graves in lots that were already sold. On top of that, they said it wouldn't affect City Cemetery at all, because the lots there weren't for sale.

After signing the ordinance, Sutro said it was only a matter of time before the cemeteries were removed, given how densely populated the western neighborhoods of San Francisco had become. And he agreed with locals who said the cemeteries were bad for people's health.

> *Any authority on sanitation will tell you that cemeteries cannot avoid being a menace to the health and lives of the cities in which they are allowed to exist. The rain soaking through the ground gets into the water supply and is bound to poison it. The air, too, is laden with deadly gasses that are detrimental to health, and in the case of San Francisco the danger is particularly great owing to the fact that the prevailing winds for the larger portion of the year blow directly into the populous City.*[231]

Sutro served a two-year term as San Francisco's mayor, from 1895 to 1897. He died of unknown causes in August 1898, although his family said he'd been in mental decline for almost a year before his death.[232] He didn't live to see the removal of the cemeteries he hated so much. In one final irony, Sutro's body was cremated, and his ashes were buried on his Sutro Heights estate next door to City Cemetery.[233]

THE END OF THE CEMETERY

By 1893, 18,000 people were buried in City Cemetery, and when San Francisco ultimately banned burials in the early 1900s, the cemetery held about 20,000 graves. Through its years as a cemetery, though, City Cemetery welcomed as many as 28,000 to 29,000 burials, including the graves of more than 6,300 Chinese residents whose bones were eventually returned to China.

A decade after Sutro's death, in December 1908, the city's health committee asked the board of supervisors to order removal of the graves at City Cemetery. The city sent notices to fraternal and other organizations that held plots to let them know eviction was on the horizon.[234] However, city officials didn't bother to disinter and relocate the indigent dead who'd been buried there on the city's dime, and many of the other remains buried at City Cemetery had nobody to claim them. While San Francisco's other cemeteries at least made an effort to move their graves to new burial grounds in Colma, City Cemetery made little effort on behalf of its dead.

Also in December 1908, San Francisco coroner Thomas Leland and Supervisor Henry Payot visited City Cemetery to investigate reports that many of the graves had become exposed and desecrated. A massive slab covering the tomb of a Russian woman named Mary Gribbish had been broken and pried away, leaving her expensive clothes and jewelry vulnerable to robbery. Vandals had dumped rubbish on other exposed graves.[235]

A year later, in December 1909, the city officially dedicated City Cemetery lands for "the most picturesque park in the world." The new park would rest on two hundred acres of coastal land, including the City Cemetery and adjacent property, bounded by Thirty-Third Avenue, Clement Street, Baker Beach and the line of West Clay Street, if it had continued through the park.[236] The *San Francisco Call* claimed that the cemetery had been closed for twenty years (it had only been eight), and yet the burials still needed to be moved. Once that happened, "the improvement of the park with drives, walks, benches and other conveniences, including lawns and flower beds, can easily be accomplished." Instead, those improvements went forward on top of thousands of now-unmarked graves.

City leaders named the new park after President Abraham Lincoln, partly because it was near the western end of the Lincoln Highway, the first highway that ran all the way across the United States. But plans to turn the land into a public park quickly changed direction. As early as 1902, golfers had established a small golf course on the site, which was expanded to have

Left: The Ladies' Seaman's Friends Society monument in City Cemetery, now Lincoln Park Golf Course. *Beth Winegarner.*

Below: The inscription on the Ladies' Seaman's Friends Society monument. *Beth Winegarner.*

fourteen holes by 1914 and a full eighteen holes by 1917, sprawling across the graveyard.[237] Lincoln Park Golf Course was the first public golf course in San Francisco and one of the first in the western United States, meaning it's open to the public without requiring membership to a country club or other private organization. It's also open to parkgoers and hikers, but they're warned to stay off the course and to watch out for flying golf balls.

Historians aren't certain how many graves remain at City Cemetery. Researcher Alex Ryder, who conducted an extensive tally of the cemetery's burials and disinterments, believes it's at least ten thousand but is probably closer to twenty thousand or more.[238]

In December 1921, as crews began excavating to build the Palace of the Legion of Honor, the forgotten dead began to make themselves known. The museum was funded by Alma de

Alma de Bretteville Spreckels, the force behind the San Francisco Legion of Honor, photographed in 1900. *Bain News Service photograph collection, Library of Congress.*

Bretteville Spreckels and her husband, Adolph, who made his money through sugar plantations and breeding racehorses, and it was intended as a memorial to California soldiers killed in World War I. When workers broke ground on the new project, they tore open 1,500 graves in the indigent section.[239]

"The site of the $250,000 memorial to the dead was once a cemetery. It still is, but the bones are now scattered. In the excavation work for the memorial workmen have uncovered about 1500 skeleton-filled coffins," reporter Vid Larsen wrote for the *Daily News*. "No provision was made for the reburying of the bodies. Workmen have cut down about nine or 10 feet in their work. Sometimes as many as four or five bodies have been pulled out in an hour."

Larsen and a colleague visited the site and reported seeing "piles of bones not completely covered by the dirt," many coffins cut in half by the teeth of excavating machines and more coffins poking out from the soil along the bluff. Someone made off with thirty-five dollars from one coffin, and someone else found an expensive ring in another. Local colleges bought some of the skulls. The foreman told the reporters that his crews refused to touch the bones, saying, "The only thing we can do is to scrape them over and cover them up again."

The Legion of Honor Museum in 1927, just a few years after it opened. *Genthe photograph collection, Library of Congress, Prints and Photographs Division.*

C.W. Eastin, an attorney representing the plot holders, told the *Daily News* the next day that the actions of Legion of Honor crews were a violation of the same laws Adolph Sutro flouted decades earlier. "Section 290 of the penal code says: Every person who mutilates, disinters or removes from the place of sepulchre the dead body of a human being without authority of the law, is guilty of a felony," Eastin told the newspaper. He added that "there is grave doubt that building a war memorial or even the public golf links at Lincoln park is legal." But his protests failed to stop the construction.

The Palace of the Legion of Honor was opened to the public on Armistice Day, November 11, 1924. The graves beneath it remained relatively undisturbed until 1993, when a new round of excavations at the museum uncovered what archaeologist Miley Holman called a "charnel heap," a mass grave likely left over from the 1921 reburials.[240] The remains belonged mostly to working-class white people who were buried in redwood coffins. Their bones showed fractures, skeletal trauma, arthritis and other signs of the heavy labor they'd performed in life. Some of the bones bore signs of medical experimentation after death. Even in 1993, the museum's officials and builders didn't want to deal with the work of processing the remains; Museum Director Harry Parker complained to the *San Francisco Chronicle* that the delays associated with the discovery would cost $50,000 a month. Ultimately, the Legion of Honor Museum turned the remains of about 900 early San Franciscans over to the medical examiner's office, and they were reinterred in Skylawn Memorial Park in Colma. The rest, however, are still beneath and around the museum, where more than 170,000 patrons visited in 2021.[241]

"These are already the bodies that no one wants; immigrants, poor people, religious minorities. It gets clearer by the minute that the city still doesn't fucking want them. To this day, the bodies of the men and women who built this city lie anonymously under a golf course and museum," writes Courtney Minick, the creator of *Here Lies a Story*. She argues that City Cemetery isn't a *former* cemetery—it's a *current* one.

In recent years, City Cemetery's legacy has attracted the attention of historians and city leaders, particularly those in Chinese communities around San Francisco. After urging from those leaders, the San Francisco Board of Supervisors granted the site landmark status in October 2022, recognizing the site's history as a graveyard for the city's immigrant and indigent dead.

Chinese community members gathered at the Kong Chow monument for the autumn festival of Chung Yeung in 2021 and 2022, bringing offerings of incense, paper money and food for the ancestors. It was probably the first time in more than a century that Chinese locals commemorated the dead at City Cemetery. "Li Dianbang (李殿邦), director of the Historical and Cultural Relics Committee of the CCBA, remarked that commemorating the Kong Chow structure could help with the current prevalence of hate crimes against Asian communities because '[a]ll ethnic groups must know each other's history and respect each other's contributions to this land,'" city archaeologist Kari Hervey-Lentz wrote.[242] Those who visit the site now may discover fresh flowers on the altar and a broom for sweeping out the Kong Chow structure, acts meant to honor the dead.

"This place has been a resting place for our earlier immigrants....Many of them did not go home, and they made America their home," said Larry Yee, president of the Chinese Consolidated Benevolent Association. "And they buried their bones here, in America."[243]

Even as San Francisco established itself as a permanent and ever-growing city, burial grounds continued to crop up whenever and wherever they were needed. These were less haphazard and "impromptu" than the city's earliest graveyards, and some of them appeared in places that have been almost entirely forgotten since. Their histories and locations may come as a surprise.

9

SCATTERED GRAVES

Yerba Buena Island Cemetery

Edward Lindsey, an English sea captain, was the first to be buried in the small cemetery on the eastern side of Yerba Buena island when he died in August 1852 aboard the brig *Palmyra* of a heart attack.[244] Lindsey was born in 1814 or 1815 in England, and in his younger years, he was hired by the English government to transport prisoners, including the first group of female prisoners who were shipped to Tasmania. He married Georgiana Minden Wilton, and they settled in Australia, where they had six children. But in 1850, he uprooted them all to cash in on the California gold rush.

After settling in San Francisco, Lindsey's family took several trips from the young city to Yerba Buena Island, about three miles northeast of the main port of San Francisco. He fell in love with the remote, wooded island and asked to be buried there when he died. During his thirty-eighth year, he got his wish. According to *San Francisco Chronicle* reporter Neil Hitt, "The funeral procession from San Francisco was a long boat bearing the body and rowed by four intimate friends, and a long line of ships' boats loaded with sorrowing friends and relatives."[245]

Lindsey's son, also named Edward, joined him in the small Yerba Buena graveyard three years later in January 1855, when he died at the age of seventeen. Over the next fifty or so years, ninety-six others would rest beside them in this burial plot, marked by "pitiful little wooden crosses, hardly

Yerba Buena Island Lighthouse buildings sometime before 1933. A small cemetery was established on the island. *Historic American Buildings Survey, Library of Congress.*

bigger than crossed lathing sticks," Hitt wrote. After the U.S. Military began using the island as an outpost in 1870, the bodies of sailors and marines became the dominant burials on Yerba Buena. Each year on Memorial Day, schoolchildren would gather white marguerite daisies, which grew abundantly on the island, and scatter them on the graves.[246] Daisies often represent love, peace, innocence and rebirth, which was probably why they were chosen for this tradition.[247]

Yerba Buena's sister island, Treasure Island, was built in the late 1930s in preparation for the 1939 Golden Gate International Exhibition, which prompted cleanup and construction on Yerba Buena. In the course of all this work, crews found a mammoth tusk believed to be more than 250,000 years old, along with the bones of indigenous peoples who'd lived on the island. Workers also removed two rows of eucalyptus trees that had shaded the cemetery, and Charles Edison, an assistant secretary of the navy, talked with other naval officials about whether the cemetery itself should be moved or removed. Some say the leadership thought the "small, ramshackle cemetery was an eyesore," so they pulled up headstones and tossed them into San Francisco Bay.[248]

Ultimately, the graves of Edward Lindsey, both senior and junior, were relocated to the San Francisco National Cemetery in the Presidio just before the exhibition took place on Treasure Island.[249] They share a small white headstone, where the engravers not only got the elder Lindsey's middle initial wrong (it says "I.," but it should be an "F." for Frederick) but also his year of death. It says 1842, when he died in 1852. If the Lindseys' remains were moved, it's likely that the rest of the graves went to the National Cemetery, too, but city officials were unwilling to share archaeological records on the site, citing privacy concerns.

St. Michael's Cemetery

Reverend Mother Baptist Russell of the Catholic Order of Our Lady of Mercy was born Katherine Russell in County Down, Ireland, in 1827 or 1828.[250] When she was nineteen she joined the Sisters of Mercy, nursing patients through Ireland's cholera epidemic of 1849. She arrived in San Francisco with a group of her Catholic sisters and Reverend Hugh Gallagher in December 1854, living in a six-room cottage on Vallejo Street. The local Sisters of Mercy were busy from the start: they opened a day school, which they called the Magdalen Asylum, in 1856, and later that year, "the first penitent [sex worker] was received and given a home."

The sisters opened St. Mary's Hospital on Stockton Street in 1857, which has become the longest-running hospital in San Francisco, now located on Stanyan Street. In 1858, they took charge of the San Francisco pesthouse, located on Twenty-Sixth Street near De Haro Street, and cared for patients during the smallpox epidemic. During this time or soon after, they purchased the county hospital on Potrero Avenue, which is now the much-larger Zuckerberg San Francisco General Hospital.

The nuns established a larger space for the Magdalen Asylum just north of the county hospital on Potrero Avenue near Twenty-First Street. Reverend Mother Russell and her sisters established the institution to help "abandoned and dissolute females." One such girl was a fourteen-year-old found by a police officer shivering in her nightgown on Kearny Street in late November 1863. "The girl is another victim of man's baser passions," a *Daily Alta California* reporter wrote. The officer knew the girl, but the traumatized teen didn't recognize the officer. She was cared for and taken to Magdalen Asylum to recuperate.[251]

The Magdalen Grotto, built in 1914, is all that remains of the original Magdalen Asylum and St. Michael's Cemetery. *Beth Winegarner.*

Places like the Magdalen Asylum—which was part of the same system that established the punitive Magdalen Laundries in Ireland—often straddled the line between offering refuge to women and girls who needed care and imprisoning teen girls against their will. Over time, the Magdalen Asylum leaned toward the latter, becoming a state-sponsored prison that incarcerated girls who had been sentenced by local courts to attend the city's industrial school, a reform school located near the intersection of San Jose and Ocean Avenues.[252] The asylum operated until 1932, though it changed its name to St. Catherine's Home and Industrial School in 1904.[253]

By 1898, the sisters were caring for about 120 people in the Old Ladies' Home they ran, along with 140 girls in Magdalen Asylum and a "large number" of patients in the hospital.

The sisters opened St. Michael's Cemetery behind the Magdalen Asylum at the corner of today's San Bruno Avenue and Twenty-First Street in May 1867. It was a "high-fenced and wooded enclosure," where the graves were marked by simple wood crosses carved with the names of the dead—"No broken columns, nor urns of bronze, nor marble slabs inscribed with the virtues of the deceased."[254] Several members of the Sisters of Mercy were buried here after their deaths, as were "penitent women who died in the asylum."

Reverend Mother Baptist Russell fell ill in the summer of 1898, when she became paralyzed and remained in bed. In early August, she died at the age of seventy. Her cause of death was determined to be "aneurysm of the arteries of the brain." She was placed in a black coffin, which remained on display in St. Mary's Church for a handful of days before she was buried in St. Michael's Cemetery.

She was not the only Sister of Mercy buried in the cemetery. Others included Sister Mary Brendan O'Sullivan in August 1888; Sister Mary Theresa King in December 1892; Mother Superior Gabriel in June 1897; Sister Mary Augustine Crofts in March 1900; and Sister Alphonsus Reilly and Sister Mary Peter O'Connor, both in June 1901. Most were originally from Ireland. We know their names because their funeral notices ran in local newspapers. Unfortunately, those newspapers didn't print funeral notices for the girls who died in the asylum or who might have been buried in St. Michael's Cemetery.

According to a disinterment register from the asylum, the St. Michael's graves were removed to a plot in Holy Cross Cemetery in Colma. But there's at least one other burial unaccounted for: that of a twelve-year-old indigenous girl named in the asylum register as Hannah Providence and in San Francisco burial records as only Hannah. Born in California, she died on March 10, 1872, of tuberculosis. According to city burial records, she was laid to rest in the Magdalen Asylum Cemetery. But she isn't mentioned in the asylum's disinterment records.[255] And because the city's burial records are incomplete for these years, it's difficult to know if any others were left out.

LAKE MERCED

When San Francisco began thinking about moving its big cemeteries out of the Richmond District, some locals suggested establishing a new cemetery near Lake Merced. Like many other cemetery spots, at the time, it was remote and rural, and nobody expected it to become a populated area anytime soon. In 1868, Archbishop Joseph Alemany purchased four hundred acres of the Rancho Laguna de la Merced, recognizing that Calvary Cemetery was filling up fast and that soon, the Catholic churches of San Francisco would need somewhere new to bury their dead.[256] It seemed like an ideal

The original planting of large-mouthed black bass in Lake Merced on October 28, 1933, after the development of a nearby cemetery was halted. *California Department of Fish and Game, Flickr's "The Commons."*

spot; it was far from populated areas, south of the city limits at that time and very close to the Southern Pacific Railroad tracks, which made it easy to transport the dead to the site.

In 1873, the board of supervisors approved a measure allowing a cemetery to open near Lake Merced. But the decision was controversial; at the time, the lake was viewed as a valuable source of fresh drinking water for the city, and the idea of having the remains of the dead so nearby horrified many locals.

Lake Merced possessed "a never-failing supply of the purest kind of water, proved by careful and many repeated analyses, to be all that is desirable. And it is abundant. The lake contains, by estimate, fourteen hundred million of gallons of water, and could, by comparatively little work, by a little ditching and other aids, be made to hold and furnish, if needed, twice that amount of water," according to the *Daily Alta California*. Any nearby burials could ruin all this: "the drainage of the graves may find its way into the Lake and unfit the water for any decent use," the *Daily Alta California* wrote, urging Mayor William Alvord to veto plans for burials here.[257]

Mayor Alvord did just that. His vote was sustained by six members of the board of supervisors but opposed by six others.[258] It wasn't enough, and burials began on the Bishop's Tract near the southern line of Lake Merced not long after. The location of this burial ground is hard to pin down, but Reverend Father Peter Gray, the rector of St. Patrick's Church, told a *San*

Francisco Examiner reporter that it was about a half mile to three-quarters of a mile from the edge of Lake Merced, that the Southern Pacific Railroad line was on the cemetery's eastern border and that the burial ground was bisected by a waterway that fed into the lake. This would put it near the northern edge of today's Lake Merced Golf Club's course. By April 1885, seven local Catholics were buried here. Reverend Gray expected the rest of the burial plots in the new cemetery to be sold within the year and that it would open "for general use" by 1886, if not sooner.[259]

But the potential for contaminating the water supply still troubled many city officials. In May 1885, a city grand jury recommended that the city issue an order forbidding further burials near Lake Merced and, ideally, moving the existing graves somewhere else.

"Now that the number of persons interred in the cemetery is small, the difficulty can easily be dealt with by securing a discontinuance of the interments and a change in the location of the cemetery; but at a future day this would be a matter of such difficulty that it would be easier to abandon the lake as a source of municipal water supply and go elsewhere, at great cost and trouble," the *Daily Alta California* reported. Allowing the slopes near Lake Merced to "become a thickly covered burial place would be insane folly."[260]

A few weeks after the grand jury issued its findings, a San Francisco health officer reported that he didn't think the burial ground would be used "to any further extent."[261]

A couple of weeks after that, that health officer and two doctors on the board of health visited the Bishop's Tract Cemetery and learned that the burial ground was, indeed, within the Lake Merced Watershed. They discovered that 315 acres of the 400-acre site drained directly into the lake.[262] Following the visit, city officials filed an order barring any further burials on the site. In September 1886, the land purchased by Catholic leaders for a cemetery by the lake went up for sale again.[263]

It's not clear what happened to these seven graves after the land was sold. It's possible they were moved to Colma; Colma's major Catholic cemetery, Holy Cross, was opened in 1887.

UNDER THE LONG BRIDGE, POTRERO HILL

This last site was never intended as hallowed ground, but when enough dead wind up in one place, they make hallowed ground on their own.

The view from San Francisco's Long Bridge, date unknown. *New York Public Library, Robert N. Dennis collection of stereoscopic views/United States/States/California/stereoscopic views of the San Francisco waterfront.*

In early December 1886, a boy named George Babbitt discovered human bones beneath the east end of Long Bridge, which once bordered the eastern edge of the Potrero neighborhood, all the way from Fourth Street to Hunters Point. Babbitt contacted the Potrero Police Station, and an officer came out to gather up the bones, which appeared to belong to a young child.[264] Locals immediately wondered if they could be the remains of Arthur Frazer, a four-year-old boy who'd gone missing near Folsom and Sixth Streets eight months earlier.

However, as investigators continued their search, they found more remains. At first, they thought the bones belonged to five different people, perhaps a group of Chinese residents who had drowned in a severe storm the previous January.[265] Then the bones of sixteen more people emerged from the mud beneath Long Bridge.[266] Ultimately, the partial skeletons represented at least twenty-four people.[267]

"The mud is said to be literally thick with them, and it is impossible to state how many may yet remain there," the *San Francisco Examiner* reported.[268]

> *They made no attempt to secure any but the largest, leaving scores of the smaller fragments lying untouched in the mud. Among those recovered are thirty-two femurs, or thigh-bones, any quantity of ribs, several shoulder-blades and five skulls. One of the skulls is perforated with a clean-cut hole, which could only have been made by a pistol ball. The bones are apparently of all ages. Some have evidently been lying in the mud for years, while upon others flesh is still adhering, and it has plainly been but a short time since they formed portions of the frameworks of living men.*

City Coroner C. O'Donnell theorized that the remains belonged to people who died in the City and County Hospital and were "thrown into the bay in order to save burial expenses," the *Daily Alta California* reported in mid-December.[269] "It is much more likely, however, that they were taken there from some dissecting room, as several bones were found to be sawed through." The *Examiner* agreed, remarking that "some of the bones show traces of having been operated upon with the saw and other surgical instruments."[270]

O'Donnell ordered an inquest into the remains, hoping to discover who they belonged to and how they wound up in the Long Bridge mud, but reporting on the results of any such investigation has been difficult to find. What an awful end to at least two dozen people who, most likely, already existed on the margins of society.

This exploration of San Francisco's forgotten cemeteries began with the Mission San Francisco de Asís, which largely managed to hold onto its burials when so many others were forced south. Now, it's time to explore the Presidio, the mission's military sibling on the northern border of San Francisco. Most of its dead remain in place, too, including those in burial grounds devoted to soldiers, seafarers and animal companions.

10

A LAND APART

CEMETERIES OF THE PRESIDIO

Juan Bautista de Anza was born in July 1736 in New Spain (Mexico), the son and grandson of military leaders. Following the family tradition, he rose through the military ranks in Nuevo España, and in 1772, the year he turned thirty-six, he led the first of several expeditions into what is now Arizona and California. De Anza proposed the foray, and Spanish leaders approved in the hope of beating the Russians in colonizing California.

De Anza headed north again in early 1776 with Father Pedro Font and a party of twelve others. They followed an inland track to the San Francisco Bay that had been carved out just six years earlier, after Spaniards got fed up with the difficult coastal route. On March 25, De Anza wrote that the party had "arrived at the arroyo of San Joseph Cupertino (now Stevens Creek), which is useful only for travelers. Here we halted for the night, having come eight leagues [about twenty-four miles] in seven and a half hours. From this place we have seen at our right the estuary which runs from the port of San Francisco." Three days later, De Anza identified the sites where the Mission San Francisco de Asís and the El Presidio Real de San Francisco would stand.

Soon after, José Joaquín Moraga, De Anza's second in command, got to work setting up the military outpost. Born in 1745, Moraga was just thirty-one when he led the development of these 1,480 acres on the northern coast of San Francisco, the area chosen for its strategic location overlooking the Golden Gate. Though it changed hands several times, this spot remained a military post for more than two hundred years, until 1994. To this day, it's

The Presidio barracks, date unknown. A small burial ground was located about where the photographer was standing. *Historic American Buildings Survey, Library of Congress.*

managed by federal agencies, legally separate from the city even though it's located within San Francisco city limits.

As the Spanish military moved in, these newcomers utterly changed the landscape of the Presidio. Most of the vegetation was cut down for building materials and fuel, and herds of cattle and other domesticated animals took over the newly cleared acreage. Spaniards carved the first major roads into the earth, including one that was probably the precursor to today's Lincoln Boulevard.[271] They built barracks and other structures and generally made themselves at home.

Such a massive military operation also meant finding places to bury the dead. Over time, four cemeteries sprung up in different parts of the Presidio, each with a very different story.

SPANISH-MEXICAN OR SPANISH-INDIAN CEMETERY

In 1820, control of the Presidio passed to Mexico, and the U.S. Military took over in 1848. But it looks like these early residents may have shared their burial grounds. The earliest such site at the Presidio was the Spanish-Mexican Cemetery on or near the Main Post of the Presidio.[272]

The names of those buried here are probably lost to history, but other details have survived. A government report on the history of the Presidio says this cemetery was located at the northwest corner of the main parade grounds, which puts it near where Montgomery Street and Lincoln Boulevard intersect today. Some of the earliest maps of the area, drawn up by the U.S. Army, identify it as a "Spanish and Indian Cemetery," rather than Spanish and Mexican. It may have included all of the above—and some U.S. soldiers, too.

It was located some distance away from the main Presidio settlement, particularly its chapel, which the author of a 2011 cultural report found unusual for a Presidio graveyard.[273] "Routinely, the dead were interred in sanctified grounds near established presidio chapels or mission churches," and this one wasn't. However, "One might speculate that the dramatic views to the bay from this point on the bluff may have influenced the decision to locate the burial ground here."

The report also notes that it's unclear how the cemetery was handled by the U.S. Army as it built Laundress' Quarters along this block of Montgomery Street in the mid-1800s or a row of barracks that later replaced them. Today, those barracks are occupied by a boutique hotel, the Lodge at the Presidio, as well as the Walt Disney Family Museum and the Society of

The Presidio's Chapel of Our Lady, located on Moraga Avenue at the end of Mesa Street, date unknown. *Historic American Buildings Survey, Library of Congress.*

California Pioneers. The cemetery was most likely located beneath where the lodge stands today. Although no aboveground sign of the burial ground remains, Presidio officials, as recently as 2011, identified it as a site where archaeological items (implying human remains, coffins or grave goods) might be found if someone went digging. City archaeologist Kari Hervey-Lentz says there's little evidence that these Spanish-era burials were removed.[274]

In July 1922, thirty-eight bodies were discovered "in an isolated spot of the Presidio," the *Chronicle* reported in 1936.[275] "The bones are believed [to be] the remains of early Spanish conquistadores who founded the local fortification." Unfortunately, the reporter didn't share any details, including who made the discovery or where the remains were found. The article implies that the graves were moved to the National Cemetery. That may have happened, but others could remain beneath the lodge and the main parade ground, where many people come to get married, get away for the weekend or picnic on the manicured lawns overlooking the San Francisco Bay.

San Francisco National Cemetery

The man who fell in love with San Francisco's landscapes after losing two battles at Bull Run, Major General Irvin McDowell, was born in Columbus, Ohio, in October 1818. His parents were Abram Irvin McDowell—later the mayor of Columbus—and Eliza Selden McDowell (née Lord), about whom little is known. The younger McDowell was lucky enough to attend the College de Troyes in France, and he graduated from the U.S. Military Academy in 1838. After college, he taught tactics at West Point and served as an aide-de-camp during the Mexican-American War.

As the American Civil War kicked off, McDowell was given command of the Union Army of Northeast Virginia in May 1861. After leading an embarrassing defeat at the First Battle of Bull Run, he served as division commander of the Army of the Potomac and was promoted to major general of volunteers. He was also blamed for the disastrous Second Battle of Bull Run, a Confederate victory in which fourteen thousand Union soldiers died. McDowell's troops allegedly hated him; many thought he was in cahoots with the Confederacy.

After the war, McDowell commanded the U.S. Army's Department of the Pacific for a while but retired from military service in 1882. He found a new purpose in landscaping and became San Francisco's park commissioner, a position in which he helped design parts of the Presidio and Golden Gate Park. He was still in that role when he died of a heart attack on May 4, 1885, at the age of sixty-six.

McDowell's funeral was one of the most significant early services held in San Francisco's National Cemetery, established just a year earlier. His pallbearers (including California governor and senator Leland Stanford) first gathered at McDowell's home on Van Ness Avenue and loaded his massive, handsome rosewood coffin into a waiting hearse. At the Central Avenue entrance to the Presidio, the funeral cortège was met by dozens of troops, who led the procession to the National Cemetery as "a chilling fog came up out of the sea and swept across the pathway of the marching troops like a vast and gloomy pall."[276] McDowell's casket was lowered into his grave, there was a sixteen-gun salute and he was remembered for his "forbearance and dignity under misfortune." He was the first major general to be buried on the West Coast.

After the U.S. Military set up shop in the Presidio in the 1840s, it established a small cemetery for its own dead. It, too, was located near the Main Post, this time on a hillside west of the parade grounds. The nine-and-a-half-acre graveyard, which was located much closer to the Presidio chapel than the Spanish-Mexican one, was ultimately absorbed into a much larger military burial ground.

The American Civil War resulted in massive casualties—about 620,000—and the survivors struggled to bury them all. Many who died on battlefields were buried hastily and anonymously, because shipping their bodies home was impractical, both financially and biologically (the Civil War also sparked the trend of embalming corpses so they could stay fresh longer before burial). In 1862, the U.S. Congress established a chain of so-called national cemeteries for the Civil War dead. The first was established in Alexandria, Virginia, and by the end of 1862, fourteen national cemeteries dotted the eastern states, from Illinois to Kentucky. Washington, D.C.'s Arlington National Cemetery, the most famous, opened in 1864.

Initially, national cemeteries were reserved for Civil War dead, but veterans began clamoring to be buried alongside their fallen brothers. Wives and families later became eligible, too.[277] Today, the country's 172 national cemeteries hold more than four million dead.

San Francisco National Cemetery was opened in 1884, wrapping itself around the nine-and-a-half-acre hillside cemetery established earlier. These early grave sites are still easy to pick out; many of the headstones are unique

The San Francisco National Cemetery. *Beth Winegarner.*

and resemble traditional grave markers of the late nineteenth century, before national cemeteries began using the identical marble or granite stones common today.

When a *Chronicle* reporter visited the National Cemetery in 1936, he described it as being "halfway up the slope on one of the Presidio hills, with a vista that sweeps down the tumbling terrain to the waters of the bay and beyond to the sheer cliffs of the Marin shore" and surrounded by a grove of trees.[278]

By 1936, 15,369 veterans and their family members had been buried in this coastal cemetery, and by 2009, those numbers had jumped to 28,952. As of this writing, in 2022, the cemetery is not taking new internments, although there is still space for people who already purchased plots for themselves or their families.

A number of big-name military men are laid to rest here, including Lieutenant General Hunter Liggett and Rear Admiral Oscar W. Farenholt, who rose from seaman to rear admiral in the U.S. Navy; Major General William R. Shafter, a veteran of the Spanish-American war; Major General Frederick Funston, who policed the city at the time of the 1851 fire; William M. Caldwell, who was killed in 1930 while escorting the Japanese instrument of ratification of the London naval treaty across the United States; and

Major Thomas Cowan Bell, a soldier, journalist, educator and founder of the Sigma Chi fraternity at Miami University in Oxford, Ohio.

The National Cemetery also houses a mass grave, where hundreds of anonymous military dead were buried. "In 1934, the Army consolidated unknown remains on this site from the former Main Post cemetery, as well as individuals removed from cemeteries at abandoned forts and camps elsewhere along the Pacific coast and western frontier. The exact number of unknowns contained at this site is uncertain—Army documents from the period differ in their accounting—but the number is between 300–500," according to Les A. Melnyk, chief spokesman for the National Cemetery Association Department within Veterans Affairs. The spot is marked with a large granite stone carved with an eagle that carries arrows and laurel leaves in its talons. On its chest is a shield that reads, "To the unknown soldier dead," and the Chi-Rho symbol, representing Christ.

However, there may still be more unidentified dead buried elsewhere in the cemetery. "Many soldiers and sailors who died overseas serving in the Philippines, China and other areas of the Pacific Theater are interred in San Francisco National Cemetery, but we are not certain if any of these were unknowns who are among those interred at this site," Melnyk said.[279]

The San Francisco National Cemetery remains one of the only visibly marked burial grounds in the city, where loved ones and descendants of the dead can visit their graves. That's largely because it was managed by the United States government for so long and wasn't beholden to the city's ban on burials in the early 1900s. But not every federal-run burial ground was so well protected.

U.S. MARINE HOSPITAL CEMETERY

Nels Anderson was born in 1878 and took up the sailor's life as a young man. The blond-haired, blue-eyed Norwegian lived a brief life and died in late 1903, far from home, of tuberculosis at the U.S. Marine Hospital in San Francisco's Presidio. French sailor Albert Green met a similar fate in June 1901, when tuberculosis and malarial fever took him at the age of twenty-seven. Likewise, Gustaf Johnson, a Russian sailor, succumbed to tuberculosis at the hospital in November 1900, after a month of convalescence. He was thirty-eight. Anderson, Green and Johnson were buried behind the hospital, along with more than eight hundred others from around the world.

The U.S. Marine Hospital Cemetery is now an area of restored coastal dunes. Its grave markers have been removed. *Beth Winegarner.*

In its earliest settler years, San Francisco served largely as a seaport for ships passing through and soon realized it needed a place where sailors could receive medical care. The first marine hospital was built just south of downtown San Francisco at Rincon Point, but a large earthquake in 1868 damaged the structure, forcing it to close.

The construction of a new marine hospital in the Presidio began in 1874 and was wrapped up in 1875, when it began to take in ailing sailors who arrived on local shores from all over the globe. Like its predecessor at Rincon Point, the new hospital established a cemetery for those who were not lucky enough to recover. More than 830 mariners were buried in the ground behind the hospital between 1875 and 1912.[280]

A *San Francisco Call* reporter visited the cemetery in 1896, describing it as a "romance of little mounds…in a valley dreary with stunted growths and hummocks of half-tamed sand dunes," where, by then, roughly two hundred were laid to rest.[281] Each was marked with a white post bearing a name and date of death, and the grounds were surrounded by fences and clusters of flowers, particularly California poppies and baby blue eyes. "The place is very wild indeed, secluded from worldly sight by kindly hills and groves and unknown only to an occasional pedestrian who leaves the beaten path for the

Presidio hills. With all its wildness the mounds and the white boards within its rugged borders contain many a romantic story," the reporter wrote.

"In those days, sailors were outcasts, men with no families, who worked long hours under brutal conditions. A look at the cemetery records of the Marine Hospital shows that most of the dead were young. Many were in their 20s," *Chronicle* reporter Carl Nolte wrote in 2006. "Most of the deaths were the result of respiratory diseases, like tuberculosis." As many as 80 percent of the sailors buried here were from countries outside the United States.[282]

Hospital records from 1894 show that, of the fifty-six sailors who perished in the marine hospital that year, fifty-four died of diseases; only two died of injuries. Among them, seventeen succumbed to tuberculosis, one of the most common fates for the hospital's patients. Despite common stereotypes, only one died of scurvy.[283] Others lost their lives to diseases of the nervous, circulatory, respiratory and digestive systems. "As a rule, Jack finds his last resting place ashore, and…the number who go to Davy Jones are infinitely in the minority," the *Call* wrote of the sailors.

Apparently, American sailors could be buried in the marine hospital cemetery for free, but noncitizens had to pay six dollars for the same privilege before 1884; that year, the price rose to ten dollars. Burials at the hospital were not communicated to the city for inclusion in its reports until 1885, but historians believe that burials at the marine hospital likely began as early as 1875, when it opened.[284] The dead were dressed in their uniforms and placed in a plain redwood coffin. "There is not much ado over his interment. He is put under the sand with a board at his head, and, at least, he is with his mates," the *Call* wrote.[285]

Sailors' comrades were most often the ones who cared for the graves. The crew of one English ship gathered money from their wages to buy a grave marker and fence for their colleague, and "the day before their ship sailed for home they were out here at the grave. Then they had a photograph taken of the monument to show in England that they had done everything in their power for their shipmate," the *Call* reported. "Some of the other fences and flowers were placed there by friends of the sailors. Those people knew the men buried here and they came and put up monuments and sowed flowers upon the graves. They were all seamen, and as far as I knew had nothing in common more than a warm heart for one another."

Not all sailors who died in the marine hospital were interred in this cemetery. At least 140 were buried elsewhere, some in the Ladies' Seamen's Friends Society plot in nearby City Cemetery.[286]

The sailors in the Marine Hospital Cemetery rested silently as the world around them changed. In 1912, the marine hospital, along with the country's other marine hospitals became a Public Health Service Hospital, and in 1931, the original wooden structure was demolished and replaced.[287] A lab for investigating bubonic plague opened in 1935 and operated until at least 1947, when it was taken over by the U.S. Centers for Disease Control.[288] The hospital was expanded in 1951 but ultimately closed in 1981 as a part of the Reagan administration's budget cuts. Several proposals came forward to reuse the buildings, including one from the City and County of San Francisco to care for AIDS patients and another from the Letterman Army Medical Center to store war reserve stock. Neither of these happened, although the Chinese-American International School used a portion of the buildings in 1989.

Over the course of so many changes, officials apparently forgot about the sailors' graves on the property. Money was set aside to move them when the marine hospital closed, but that didn't happen. The cemetery was buried in ten feet of landfill in the 1930s, and the Works Progress Administration built a parking lot and tennis courts on part of the site in 1933. By the 1950s, when the hospital was expanded, the entire graveyard

A viewing area for the Marine Hospital Cemetery with the Presidio Landmark apartments in the background, where the hospital used to stand. *Beth Winegarner.*

was covered in debris and dirt, some of it from the excavation of a nearby missile site at Fort Miley.[289] At some point, it was marked on military maps as "Landfill 8." In 1990, Woodward-Clyde Consultants, working on behalf of the U.S. Army Corps of Engineers, trenched a small portion of the property with a backhoe and found graves about fifteen feet below the surface.[290]

Today, the imposing brick hospital is now a luxury apartment building, the Presidio Landmark, offering "one-of-a-kind living experiences" just a stone's throw from the Pacific Ocean. Behind it, the cemetery is still there.

Instead of relocating the graves, Presidio leaders chose to keep them at the site and surround them with restored habitat. In 2011, a new trail and viewing area opened in honor of the cemetery, featuring a wood-planked boardwalk leading to a balcony overlooking dunes, coastal scrub plants and native birds and other animals.[291] It reads, "Home is the sailor, home from the sea" (a quote from English poet Alfred Edward Houseman) and "In memory of the merchant mariners from around the world who rest here."

Presidio Pet Cemetery

No one knows for sure when this sweet little cemetery, located along McDowell Avenue and shadowed by the Highway 101 overpasses, got its start, but it probably saw its first burials in the early 1950s. At that time, the Presidio was home to about two thousand U.S. Army families, many of whom kept pets at home. Lieutenant General Joseph Swing, the commander of the Presidio from 1951 to 1954, is sometimes credited with approving the creation of the pet cemetery, but there are no official records on its history. Legends claim that the plot was once a graveyard for nineteenth-century cavalry horses or guard dogs from World War II—no one knows for sure.[292]

At least 424 beloved critters are buried here, mostly cats and dogs but also a few lizards, birds and other companions. In the 1970s, the pet cemetery fell into disrepair. "Legend has it that an anonymous former Navy man became the unofficial caretaker in those years and repaired the deteriorating headstones and repainted the fence," says the National Park Service. Handmade gravestones—many of them repaired by unknown hands—commemorate Princess Tuptim, Cupcake, Wiggles, Sammi, Mr. Twister, Raspberry, Yurikov and Mr. Iguana, among others. Today, clusters

The pet cemetery in San Francisco's Presidio. *Carol M. Highsmith Archive, Library of Congress, Prints and Photographs Division.*

of white clover and raspberry-colored geraniums twine around the graves, while native birds flit among the plants. Despite the cars roaring overhead, it's a peaceful spot.

As they have with the marine hospital cemetery, the Presidio's leaders have committed to preserving this burial ground for visitors.[293] Even Knucklehead, Sweet Alyssum and Judy, the faithful cocker spaniel, deserve to live on in future generations' minds. As one white-painted marker reads, "The love these animals gave will never be forgotten."

If only that were true for everyone still buried in San Francisco.

CONCLUSION

I am the granddaughter of two funeral directors; you could say that death is in my blood.

My dad's father, Gail Winegarner, ran the Winegarner Funeral Home in Columbus, Ohio, along with his father, William Winegarner, and took over the business when William died in November 1933. The building was set up with the funeral home on one side and the living quarters on the other and, before my dad and his brothers were born, my grandparents lived there. My grandfather once told me that, occasionally, families didn't come back to pick up the ashes of their loved ones. He always hung on to them in case someone returned to claim them later. I couldn't imagine anyone leaving their kin behind like that.

One such set of ashes somehow fell inside one of the walls of the building and got stuck. Then, in the winter of 1934, the building caught fire in the middle of the night. My grandparents ran out into the sub-zero night with only the clothes on their backs. Decades later, I'm still haunted by the thought of that poor person whose remains were burned twice.

That was the end of the Winegarner Funeral Home, but my grandfather remained in the business until at least the early 1940s. When his own grandmother Maybell Friend died in 1941, he served as her mortician. I wonder what it felt like for him to tend to his grandmother in that way after death, preparing her for the passage into the next world. He never talked about it with me or my dad; I only discovered the story when I found her obituary while researching some family history.

My mother's father was a Southern Baptist reverend, so funerals were only part of his services, but they were a regular part judging by how often his name appeared in the funeral notices in and around Atlanta. He preached and led observances at Ebenezer Baptist and Belle Isles in Atlanta, Georgia, but other times, he traveled up to fifty miles away from his home base in Smyrna to save souls and help families see their loved ones off to the afterlife.

I can't say for sure if this is why I've always been fascinated by cemeteries and the processes through which we grieve and remember our dead, but it's probably part of the mix. The silence, the carved stones, the names and brief histories have sparked my imagination since I was a teen. So, I felt a distinct lack when, in the early 2000s, I moved to San Francisco, the city famous for having no cemeteries.

When I started researching for this book, I did it because I was astonished at how many dead had been left behind during the mass exodus to Colma. But over time, what surprised me instead was how quickly San Francisco erased the memory of burial grounds that were active only a decade or two earlier. Today, few San Franciscans realize that they walk, bike or drive among existing graves every day. That feels like a real loss.

Local builders have been uncovering human remains in forgotten cemeteries since San Francisco's infancy, partly because so little was done to preserve the city's collective knowledge of them. If this keeps happening, why do we keep forgetting?

Kari Hervey-Lentz, an archaeologist working in the San Francisco Planning Department, calls what happened to the city's graveyards "obliteration," an act that cut off everyday residents from the history of the land they live on.[294] This obliteration has consequences for the living and the dead; it severs people's connections to their ancestors and history, Hervey-Lentz writes.

And worse, "Obliteration of cemeteries resulted in lost history, especially history belonging to marginalized groups that often bore the brunt of obliteration efforts," Hervey-Lentz writes. "The obliteration of cemeteries can be interpreted as a kind of violence, not solely in the destruction of physical space, but as a damage that hinders and fragments public memory." And "when these people have been disenfranchised in life, their resting places in the cemetery are often all that is left of their memory. The demolition of such spaces with no consideration for the descendant community effectively erases whatever tenuous links such disenfranchised people had to immortality."

Ultimately, it doesn't matter much whether San Francisco's dead, especially its marginalized dead, were left behind intentionally or through neglect. The result is the same: their descendants, by both blood and geography, have no way of finding and connecting with them in a tangible way. Given that these were the people who physically built the city we know as San Francisco, we are all their children of a kind, and we owe them a debt of respect.

There's another consequence for the living: "Graveyards represent spaces for grief…that have been denied so many in our modern lives," Allyson Shaw writes in *Ashes and Stones*.[295] They are one of the only places left where it's acceptable to grieve and be seen doing it, rather than brushing ourselves off and getting on with life. It doesn't matter if we visit cemeteries to mourn our own dead; the symbolism, the setting, the quiet of these spaces remind us that it's OK to remember and deeply feel our losses.

So, what can be done? Do we unearth tens of thousands of dead, attempt to identify them through scant burial records or DNA matching and try to find space for them in Colma? Not only would that be exorbitantly expensive, but it would also mean destroying huge swaths of the city to get to the graves underneath. Furnishing each plot with a new grave marker would also be costly and potentially create obstacles in places like the Legion of Honor, the Asian Art Museum and the Main Library unless they were embedded in the floors, like they are in Westminster Abbey.

San Francisco could rememorialize these places, and in some cases, it has. The city installed an informational panel in Lincoln Park in October 2022, telling visitors about the cemetery and the dead beneath their feet. The Marine Hospital Cemetery is marked with a plaque to remind passersby of the sailors resting among the dunes.

But there are many more possibilities. The Marine Hospital Cemetery could add a marker with the names of the sailors as collected by researcher Jennifer McCann in 2006. Someone could restore the plaque that once hung on the brick wall surrounding the UCSF Laurel Hill Campus, marking the Laurel Hill Cemetery boundary, which disappeared sometime before 2012. The city could add signifiers around Civic Center, USF, San Francisco General Hospital and the many "impromptu" cemetery sites that dotted today's Financial District, much in the same way it has marked the Barbary Coast Trail or the collection of Ramaytush Ohlone words along King Street.

With this book, I've worked to reidentify each former cemetery site to rebuild our understanding of these places from the ground up. I want people to visit these places and remember what they were before, as well as who might still be resting there now. I've attempted to be as complete in my research as possible, but there may yet be more undiscovered cemeteries. Archival records suggest there may be one on Sixteenth Street between Castro and Noe Streets, a Catholic cemetery just south of the Hart Jewish Cemetery at Gough and Green Streets and another at Laguna Honda Hospital.[296]

The poet Kenneth Rexroth once argued that there is "nothing underground about" San Francisco. On the contrary, it is a city with history as layered and rich as the Franciscan Complex stone that underlies it. The original home of the Ohlone people is famed for the Spanish colonizers, the gold rush, the Beats and the Summer of Love, queer and trans rights movements and the tech boom. It's also famed for having no cemeteries within its city limits, but that's clearly not the case. Many cemeteries and many dead—fifty thousand or more—are still here underground. They've just been erased—obliterated.

"The only way to deny a cemetery its role as a sacred space is to deny its existence as a cemetery, as symbolic space. When the cemetery remains a cemetery, it can still speak," writes Elizabethada A. Wright.[297] It's time to stop denying these sacred places their history and their very existence.

NOTES

Introduction

1. Find a Grave, "Forestview Cemetery."
2. Forestville Planning Association, "Early Development and People."
3. Dunning, "Burial in London."
4. Berman, "What Lies Below."
5. Shelton, "Unmaking Historic Spaces," passim.
6. Hervey-Lentz, "Remaking an Unmade Cultural Landscape."
7. SF Genealogy, "San Francisco Population."

1. Creek of Sorrows: Mission Dolores Cemetery

8. Find a Grave, "Francisca Alvarez."
9. National Park Service, "Indigenous Period."
10. Milliken, *Time of Little Choice*, passim.
11. History, "California Missions."
12. Ibid.
13. We Are Water, www.wawproject.net.
14. Kamiya, "Dolores' Dark Legacy."
15. Ruscin, *Mission Memoirs*, passim.
16. Find a Grave, "Clorinde Castillo"; Cleary, "Mission Dolores."

17. Svanevik and Burgess, *City of Souls*, passim.
18. Ibid.
19. "Streets and Highways," *Daily Alta California*, April 27, 1888.
20. "The Supervisors," *Daily Alta California*, September 25, 1888.
21. "Mission Dolores Cemetery," *Daily Alta California*, May 31, 1889.
22. "Real Estate—The Market Quiet, But a Number of Large Sales Announced," *Daily Alta California*, June 10, 1889.
23. *Daily Alta California*, June 14, 1889.
24. Ibid.
25. *San Francisco Morning Call*, June 8, 1889.
26. "Streets and Highways," *Daily Alta California*, November 15, 1889.
27. "Mission Dolores Cemetery," *Daily Alta California*, July 3, 1890.
28. John W. Blackett, "Mission Map," San Francisco Cemeteries.
29. Jackson and Yi, "Less Than Half."
30. California Missions, "San Francisco de Asís."
31. Galvan, interview with Jeff Hunt.
32. Casey, "Tekakwitha Lily."

2. Guardians of the Dead: San Francisco's Cypress Trees

33. Ovid, *Metamorphoses*, passim.
34. Ibid.
35. Sullivan, *Trees of San Francisco*, passim.
36. Carlson, email to the author.

3. "Impromptu Burials": San Francisco's Early Unofficial Cemeteries

37. Virtual Museum of the City of San Francisco, "1820s to the Gold Rush."
38. Bruner, *Old Burying Grounds*, passim.
39. Hervey-Lentz, "Remaking an Unmade Cultural Landscape."
40. "City Items," *Daily Alta California*, April 4, 1858.
41. *San Francisco Californian*, July 24, 1847.
42. *San Francisco Bulletin*, January 2, 1857.
43. *Stockton Daily Argus*, January 8, 1857.
44. "City Items," *Daily Alta California*, April 4, 1858.
45. SF Genealogy, "Telegraph Hill Cemetery."

46. FoundSF, "Old Cemeteries."

47. John W. Blackett, "Bush St. Map," San Francisco Cemeteries.

48. Hervey-Lentz, "Remaking an Unmade Cultural Landscape."

49. "Pioneers' Bones," *San Francisco Call*, February 7, 1894.

50. Bruner, *Old Burying Grounds*, passim.

51. Hervey-Lentz, "Remaking an Unmade Cultural Landscape."

52. "Human Skeleton; Found in a Decayed Coffin," *San Francisco Call*, March 16, 1902.

53. "The Public Cemetery," *Daily Alta California*, July 31, 1853.

54. John W. Blackett, "Rincon Point Map," San Francisco Cemeteries.

55. "City Items," *Daily Alta California*, February 26, 1863.

56. "City Intelligence," *Daily Alta California*, February 4, 1851.

57. Svanevik and Burgess, *City of Souls*, passim.

58. "Cemeteries," *Daily Alta California*, March 12, 1850.

59. "Local Matters," *Daily Alta California*, February 7, 1853.

60. "Powell Street Cemetery," *Daily Alta California*, May 21, 1853.

61. Jackson Fuller Real Estate, "Summit."

62. *San Francisco Daily Evening Post*, November 16, 1878.

63. "City Items," *Daily Alta California*, June 25, 1861.

4. The Heart of the City: Yerba Buena and Green Oak Cemeteries

64. SF Genealogy, "San Francisco Population."

65. Kellawan, "Normalizing Prejudice."

66. Hervey-Lentz, "Remaking an Unmade Cultural Landscape."

67. SF Genealogy, "1850, Deaths."

68. Hervey-Lentz, "Remaking an Unmade Cultural Landscape."

69. Kamiya, "When San Francisco Burned."

70. *San Francisco Chronicle*, April 9, 1908.

71. *Daily Alta California*, July 22, 1862.

72. Bruner, *Old Burying Grounds*, passim.

73. LaBounty, email to the author.

74. Daughters of the American Revolution, "San Francisco Cemetery Records."

75. SF Genealogy, "San Francisco Population."

76. Hervey-Lentz, "Remaking an Unmade Cultural Landscape."

77. "Mayor's Message," *Daily Alta California*, June 8, 1850.

78. "Common Council," *Daily Alta California*, September 16, 1852; *Daily Alta California*, October 11, 1852.

79. "Saturday Morning," *Daily Alta California*, November 19, 1853.

80. John W. Blackett, "Yerba Buena Cemetery," San Francisco Cemeteries.

81. Minick, "Lost Cemeteries of San Francisco."

82. "Wednesday Morning," *Daily Alta California*, December 7, 1853.

83. Ibid.

84. Hervey-Lentz, "Remaking an Unmade Cultural Landscape."

85. Ibid.

86. Whiting, "Foundation of Bones."

87. Sack and Siddique, "Corpses."

88. *San Francisco Chronicle*, April 9, 1908.

89. Ibid.

90. *San Francisco Chronicle*, June 9, 1932.

91. *San Francisco Chronicle*, March 8, 1934.

92. Herel, "97 Pioneers' Remains."

93. Ibid.

94. Associated Press, "Burial Place Found."

95. "City Items," *Daily Alta California*, June 25, 1861.

96. Dobrzynski, "Five Questions for Jay Xu"; SFGov, "Library Total."

97. "Local Matters," *Daily Alta California*, January 4, 1850.

98. SF Genealogy, "Green Oak Cemetery."

5. Home of Peace: San Francisco's First Jewish Cemeteries

99. Find a Grave, "Joseph Tobias Bach."

100. York and Keefe, "Great Fires."

101. Caffentzis, "FIRE!"

102. "City Intelligence," *Daily Alta California*, June 30, 1851.

103. Ibid.

104. Salvano, "San Francisco's Lost Cemeteries."

105. "City Items," *Daily Alta California*, July 27, 1860.

106. Salvano, "San Francisco's Lost Cemeteries."

107. John W. Blackett, "Dolores Park," San Francisco Cemeteries.

108. "City Items," *Daily Alta California*, April 26, 1860.

109. "City Items," *Daily Alta California*, July 26, 1860.

110. Montgomery, "Black and White History."

111. Ibid.

112. Find a Grave, "Joseph Tobias Bach."

113. Find a Grave, "Augusta G. Blaisdell Michael."

114. Ibid.

115. Revised Mission Dolores Neighborhood Survey.

116. FoundSF, "Dolores Park."

117. Flamant, "Child-Saving Charities."

118. Revised Mission Dolores Neighborhood Survey.

119. Smith, "Dolores Park."

6. The Rural Cemetery Movement Arrives: Lone Mountain and Laurel Hill Cemeteries

120. "Passengers," *Daily Alta California*, December 12, 1850.

121. "Law Courts," *Daily Alta California*, January 29, 1852.

122. Arader Galleries, "Seeing the World from Here."

123. "Wednesday Morning," *Daily Alta California*, December 7, 1853.

124. "Saturday Morning," *Daily Alta California*, December 24, 1853.

125. "Dedication of Lone Mountain—Interesting Ceremony," *Daily Alta California*, May 31, 1854.

126. "Masonic Cemetery," *Daily Alta California*, January 20, 1867.

127. Outside Lands, "Laurel Hill Cemetery."

128. Ibid.

129. *Daily Alta California*, July 22, 1862.

130. "Lone Mountain Cemetery," *Daily Alta California*, May 10, 1854.

131. "City Items," *Daily Alta California*, April 12, 1867.

132. SF Genealogy, "Laurel Hill Cemetery."

133. Ibid.

134. Hervey-Lentz, "Remaking an Unmade Cultural Landscape."

135. Ibid.

136. "The Bear Again," *Daily Alta California*, May 19, 1884.

137. "Cemetery Threatened," *San Francisco Call*, December 6, 1896.

138. Brady, "Famous American Duels."

139. "Sutter-Street Extension," *San Francisco Call*, November 28, 1896.

140. "Attorney Lawson Makes a Find," *San Francisco Call*, December 20, 1896.

141. Kusinitz, "Germ Theory."

142. "How We Bury Our Dead," *Daily Alta California*, February 5, 1868.

143. "The Street Committee," *San Francisco Call*, July 20, 1895.

144. "No Burials in the City," *San Francisco Call*, October 11, 1895.

145. Ibid.

146. "War on Cemeteries," *San Francisco Call*, October 12, 1895.

147. "Doom of the Cemeteries," *San Francisco Call*, January 31, 1896.
148. Ibid.
149. Svanevik and Burgess, *City of Souls*, passim.
150. Ibid.
151. Minick, "Lost Cemeteries of San Francisco."
152. Bevk, "Hidden Histories."
153. Hervey-Lentz, "Remaking an Unmade Cultural Landscape."
154. Ibid.
155. Noe Hill, "California Historical Landmark 760."
156. Barclay, email to the author.

7. The "Big Six": Lone Mountain's Cemetery Subdivisions

157. Advertisement, *Daily Alta California*, December 23, 1866.
158. Sawyer, "Old Calvary Cemetery Grounds."
159. Cerna, "Mystery Solved."
160. Webster, "Inflation Calculator"; "Old Point Lobos Road," *San Francisco Call*, May 6, 1895.
161. Brinklow, "San Francisco Streets"; Cantwell, "Point Lobos."
162. "Squatting on Cemetery Grounds," *Daily Alta California*, July 22, 1853.
163. "Dedication of the Odd Fellows Cemetery," *Daily Alta California*, November 27, 1865.
164. "Statutes of California," *Daily Alta California*, April 17, 1870.
165. "Odd Fellows' Cemetery Association," *Daily Alta California*, September 28, 1875.
166. *San Francisco Morning Call*, October 6, 1893.
167. *San Francisco Morning Call*, August 15, 1899.
168. "To Test Cemetery Ordinance," *San Francisco Call*, September 19, 1901.
169. Svanevik and Burgess, *City of Souls*, passim.
170. Kukura, "Grave Undertaking."
171. Rubenstein, "Little Girl."
172. Cerna, "Mystery Solved."
173. Ibid.
174. "The First Columbarium," *San Francisco Call*, August 9, 1895.
175. Rhoads, "Cemetery of the Week 30."
176. Polony, "What Is a Columbarium?"
177. Weirde, "Masons Arrive."
178. Noe Hill, "California Historical Landmark 650."

179. California, U.S., Mortuary and Cemetery Records, 1801–1932.

180. "Masonic Cemetery," *Daily Alta California*, January 20, 1867.

181. *Daily Alta California*, August 15, 1880.

182. *San Francisco Morning Call*, February 14, 1887.

183. *Masonic Cemetery Ass'n v. Gamage, 38 F.2d 950 (9th Cir. 1930)*, U.S. Court of Appeals for the Ninth Circuit—38 F.2d 950, March 10, 1930.

184. Hervey-Lentz, "Remaking an Unmade Cultural Landscape."

185. Shelton, "Unmaking Historic Spaces," n.p.

186. *San Francisco Chronicle*, December 22, 1931.

187. Fender, "Secret Tombstones."

188. Brooks, "So Many Graves in Colma?"

189. "City Items," *Daily Alta California*, August 21, 1862.

190. "City Items," *Daily Alta California*, November 11, 1860.

191. SF Genealogy, "Calvary Cemetery."

192. "More Land Troubles," *Daily Alta California*, June 22, 1869.

193. "A Grave Desecrator Fined," *Daily Alta California*, February 11, 1887.

194. "Truth of the Treasure," *San Francisco Call*, June 17, 1896.

195. "Most Weird Bedroom in San Francisco," *San Francisco Call*, November 18, 1900.

196. Minick, "Lost Cemeteries of San Francisco."

197. LaBounty, "Calvary Cemetery."

198. Hervey-Lentz, "Remaking an Unmade Cultural Landscape."

199. Ibid.

200. "The New Chinese Cemetery," *Daily Alta California*, February 8, 1877.

201. LaBounty, draft report on City Cemetery.

202. "The Russian Cemetery," *Daily Alta California*, May 31, 1888.

203. Ibid.

204. "Park or Graveyard?" *San Francisco Examiner*.

205. Mcfarlane, "Bay District Racing Track."

206. "Richmond's Goblin Horse," *San Francisco Call*, November 28, 1897.

207. Svanevik and Burgess, *City of Souls*, passim.

8. Left Behind: City Cemetery

208. *San Francisco Call*, February 18, 1882.

209. Ibid.

210. Ibid.

211. SF Genealogy, "Golden Gate Cemetery."

212. Ibid.
213. *San Francisco Chronicle*, March 20, 1890.
214. Rouse, "What We Didn't Understand," passim.
215. Tsai, *Chinese Experience*, passim.
216. Wikipedia, "Adolph Sutro."
217. Minick, "Sutro Forest."
218. Outside Lands, "Adolph Sutro."
219. "A New Ocean Road," *Daily Alta California*, August 10, 1886.
220. "Railroading in a Graveyard," *San Francisco Call*, March 17, 1895.
221. Ibid.
222. "Visit to the City Cemetery," *Daily Alta California*, September 25, 1889.
223. "Not City Property," *Daily Alta California*, September 28, 1889.
224. Ibid.
225. "The City Cemetery," *Daily Alta California*, February 3, 1891.
226. Ibid.
227. *San Francisco Examiner*, February 3, 1891.
228. "Must Be Condemned," *Daily Alta California*, February 14, 1891.
229. Wikipedia, "Fort Miley."
230. "Doom of the Cemeteries," *San Francisco Call*.
231. Ibid.
232. "Death Claims Adolph Sutro, Philanthropist," *San Francisco Call*, August 9, 1898.
233. Svanevik and Burgess, *City of Souls*, passim.
234. *San Francisco Morning Call*, December 10, 1908.
235. *San Francisco Morning Call*, December 16, 1908.
236. "Land Is Dedicated for New City Park," *San Francisco Call*, December 4, 1909.
237. Lincoln Park Golf Course.
238. Ryder, interview with the author.
239. Larsen, "City Scrapers."
240. Minick, "Lost Cemeteries of San Francisco."
241. Da Silva, "Visitor Figures 2021."
242. Hervey-Lentz, "Remaking an Unmade Cultural Landscape."
243. Yee, interview with the author.

9. Scattered Graves

244. Boyes, "Legend of Yerba Buena."

245. Neil Hitt, *San Francisco Chronicle*, September 26, 1937.
246. Ibid.
247. Minnetonka Orchards, "Marguerite Daisy."
248. Ancestry, "Captain Lindsey and Son."
249. SF Genealogy, "Yerba Buena Island Cemetery."
250. "Mother Russell Is at Rest," *San Francisco Examiner*, August 7, 1898.
251. "Court Proceedings," *Daily Alta California*, November 29, 1863.
252. Byers, "Moran on the San Francisco Magdalen Asylum"; Mcfarlane, "House of Refuge."
253. Lattin, "Magdalene Grotto."
254. "The Magdalen Asylum," *San Francisco Chronicle*, December 10, 1871.
255. Winegarner, "Hidden, Painful History."
256. *San Francisco Examiner*, April 15, 1885.
257. "Proposed Desecration of Lake Merced," *Daily Alta California*, October 17, 1873.
258. "Board of Supervisors," *Daily Alta California*, October 28, 1873.
259. "Our Water Supply," *San Francisco Examiner*, April 15, 1885.
260. "Serious Possibilities," *Daily Alta California*, May 17, 1885.
261. "The City," *Daily Alta California*, June 6, 1885.
262. "Lake Merced Cemetery," *Daily Alta California*, June 12, 1885.
263. *San Francisco Examiner*, September 17, 1886.
264. "Human Bones Found," *Daily Alta California*, December 7, 1886.
265. "The Potrero Mystery," *Daily Alta California*, December 10, 1886.
266. "The Potrero Mystery," *Daily Alta California*, December 11, 1886.
267. Hervey-Lentz, "Remaking an Unmade Cultural Landscape."
268. "More Mystery: Sixteen Additional Skeletons Unearthed," *San Francisco Examiner*, December 11, 1886.
269. "The Potrero Mystery," *Daily Alta California*, December 11, 1886.
270. "More Mystery," *San Francisco Examiner*.

10. A Land Apart: Cemeteries of the Presidio

271. Presidio Trust, "West of Main Parade."
272. John W. Blackett, San Francisco Cemeteries.
273. Presidio Trust, "West of Main Parade."
274. Hervey-Lentz, "Remaking an Unmade Cultural Landscape."
275. *San Francisco Chronicle*, February 9, 1936.
276. "The Dead Commander," *Daily Alta California*, May 7, 1885.

277. Veterans Affairs, "National Cemetery Administration."
278. *San Francisco Chronicle*, February 9, 1936.
279. Melnyk, email to the author.
280. McCann, "Marine Hospital Cemetery."
281. "Where Jack Is at Rest," *San Francisco Call*, March 29, 1896.
282. Ibid.
283. Ibid.
284. McCann, "Marine Hospital Cemetery."
285. Ibid.
286. Ibid.
287. U.S. Public Health Service Hospital (Marine Hospital) Archives, 1874–1996, National Park Service, U.S. Department of the Interior.
288. Parascandola, "MCWA to CDC," passim.
289. U.S. Public Health Service Hospital (Marine Hospital) Archives, 1874–1996, National Park Service, U.S. Department of the Interior.
290. McCann, "Marine Hospital Cemetery."
291. Presidio, "Marine Cemetery Vista."
292. National Park Service, "Presidio Pet Cemetery."
293. Presidio, "Pet Cemetery."

Conclusion

294. Hervey-Lentz, "Remaking an Unmade Cultural Landscape."
295. Shaw, *Ashes and Stones*, passim.
296. San Francisco Planning Department, "Appendix F."
297. Wright, "Rhetorical Spaces," 51–81.

BIBLIOGRAPHY

Ancestry. "Gravestone for Captain Lindsey and Son." July 30, 2014. www.ancestry.com.

Arader Galleries. "Seeing the World from Here: Lone Mountain Cemetery." www.arader.com.

Associated Press. "Burial Place Found for 97 From 1800s." February 22, 2004.

Barclay, Diane. Email to the author. February 7, 2023.

Berman, Andrew. "What Lies Below: NYC's Forgotten and Hidden Graveyards." 6sqft. December 21, 2017. www.6sqft.com.

Bevk, Alex. "Hidden Histories: Laurel Hill Cemetery." Curbed San Francisco. July 2, 2012. sf.curbed.com.

Blackett, John W. San Francisco Cemeteries. www.sanfranciscocemeteries.com.

Boyes, Marcia Edwards. "The Legend of Yerba Buena Island." SF Genealogy. www.sfgenealogy.org.

Brady, Cyrus Townsend. "Famous American Duels." *Munsey's Magazine*, August 1905.

Brinklow, Adam. "How San Francisco Streets Got Their Names." Curbed San Francisco. January 24, 2020. sf.curbed.com.

Brooks, Jon. "Why Are There So Many Graves in Colma? And So Few in San Francisco?" KQED. www.kqed.org.

Bruner, Helen Marcia. *California's Old Burying Grounds*. San Francisco, CA: National Society of Colonial Dames of America, 1945.

Byers, Phillip. "Katherine Moran on the San Francisco Magdalen Asylum." Cushwa Center. March 9, 2021. cushwa.nd.edu.

Caffentzis, Joe. "FIRE!" FoundSF. www.foundsf.org.

California, U.S., Mortuary and Cemetery Records, 1801–1932.

California Missions Foundation. "San Francisco de Asís." www.californiamissionsfoundation.org.

Cantwell, Brian J. "California's Point Lobos Is Some of Earth's Prettiest Coastline." *Seattle Times*, November 20, 2015.

Carlson, Ben. Email from Carlson, spokesman for San Francisco Friends of the Urban Forest, to the author. May 21, 2022.

Casey, Cindy. "Tekakwitha Lily of the Mohawk." Public Art and Architecture from Around the World. www.artandarchitecture-sf.com.

Cerna, Joseph. "Mystery Solved: Remains of Girl in Forgotten Casket Was Daughter of Prominent San Francisco Family." *Los Angeles Times*, May 10, 2017.

Cleary, Brother Guire. "Mission Dolores: Historical Essay." FoundSF. www.foundsf.org.

Da Silva, José. "Visitor Figures 2021: The 100 Most Popular Art Museums in the World—But Is Covid Still Taking Its Toll?" *Art Newspaper*, March 28, 2022.

Daughters of the American Revolution, California State Society, Tamalpais Chapter. "San Francisco Cemetery Records, 1848–1863." 1938.

Dobrzynski, Judith H. "Five Questions for Jay Xu, a Year After the Asian Art Museum's Near-Bankruptcy." *Arts Journal*, January 30, 2012.

Dunning, Hayley. "A History of Burial in London." Natural History Museum. www.nhm.ac.uk.

Fender, Hillary. "The Secret Tombstones of Buena Vista Park." *Hoodline*, October 21, 2013. www.hoodline.com.

Find a Grave. "Augusta G. Blaisdell Michael." www.findagrave.com.

———. "Clorinde Castillo." www.findagrave.com.

———. "Forestview Cemetery." www.findagrave.com.

———. "Francisca Alvarez." www.findagrave.com.

———. "Joseph Tobias Bach." www.findagrave.com.

Flamant, James. "Child-Saving Charities in This Big Town." *San Francisco Morning Call*, May 28, 1893.

Forestville Planning Association. "The Early Development and People of Forestville." www.forestvillefpa.org.

FoundSF. "Dolores Park—1906." www.foundsf.org.

———. "Old Cemeteries in the City." www.foundsf.org.

Galvan, Andrew. Interview with Jeff Hunt in "San Francisco Cemeteries, Part 2." *Storied: San Francisco Podcast*. October 11, 2022.

Herel, Susan. "97 Pioneers' Remains to Be Laid to Rest Again." *San Francisco Chronicle*, February 19, 2004.

Hervey-Lentz, Kari. "Remaking an Unmade Cultural Landscape: Mapping the Space and Exploring the Meaning of San Francisco's Historical Cemeteries." Master's thesis, Sonoma State University, 2022.

History. "California Missions." www.history.com.

Hitt, Neil. *San Francisco Chronicle*, September 26, 1937.

Jackson, Chris, and Jinhee Yi. "Less Than Half of Americans Believe Ghosts Are Real." Ipsos, October 24, 2019. www.ipsos.com.

Jackson Fuller Real Estate. "The Summit." www.jacksonfuller.com.

Kamiya, Gary. "Mission Dolores' Dark Legacy for Indians: From Salvation to Subjugation and Death." *San Francisco Chronicle*, November 1, 2019.

———. "When San Francisco Burned Down Six Times—In a Year and a Half." *San Francisco Chronicle*, April 16, 2021.

Kellawan, Rebecca, "Normalizing Prejudice: Gold Rush Healthcare and the Rise of Modern Hospitals in San Francisco." e-flux. November 2020. www.e-flux.com.

Kukura, Joe. "A Grave Undertaking." *SF Weekly*, September 27, 2017.

Kusinitz, Marc. "Germ Theory." Encyclopedia.com. www.encyclopedia.com.

LaBounty, Woody. "Calvary Cemetery: A Closer Look." Open SF History. www.opensfhistory.org.

———. Draft report on City Cemetery. 2022.

———. Email to the author. October 15, 2022.

Larsen, Vid. "City Scrapers Tear Open 1500 Graves in Old S.F. Cemetery." *Daily News*, December 23, 1921.

Lattin, Don. "Magdalene Grotto Still Draws Faithful." *San Francisco Chronicle*, August 24, 2003.

Lincoln Park Golf Course. www.lincolnparkgolfcourse.com.

Masonic Cemetery Ass'n v. Gamage, 38 F.2d 950 (9th Cir. 1930). U.S. Court of Appeals for the Ninth Circuit—38 F.2d 950. March 10, 1930.

McCann, Jennifer. "The Marine Hospital Cemetery, Presidio of San Francisco, California." Presidio Archaeology Center. 2006.

Mcfarlane, Angus. "Bay District Racing Track." Outside Lands. www.outsidelands.org.

———. "The House of Refuge." Outside Lands. www.outsidelands.org.

Melnyk, Les A. Email to the author. September 13, 2022.

Milliken, Randall. *A Time of Little Choice: The Disintegration of Tribal Culture in the San Francisco Bay Area 1769–1910*. Menlo Park, CA: Ballena Press Publication, 1995.

Minick, Courtney. "The Lost Cemeteries of San Francisco." Here Lies a Story. www.hereliesastory.com.

————. "Sutro Forest." Here Lies a Story. www.hereliesastory.com.

Minnetonka Orchards. "The Marguerite Daisy." www.minnetonkaorchardmn. com.

Montgomery, Kevin. "A Black and White History of Dolores Park." *Uptown Almanac*, February 25, 2011.

National Park Service. "Indigenous Period." www.nps.gov.

————. "Presidio Pet Cemetery." www.nps.gov.

Noe Hill. "California Historical Landmark 650, Site of the What Cheer House." www.noehill.com.

————. "California Historical Landmark 760, Laurel Hill Cemetery Site." www.noehill.com.

Outside Lands. "Adolph Sutro." www.outsidelands.org.

————. "Laurel Hill Cemetery." www.outsidelands.org.

Ovid. *Metamorphoses*. New York: Penguin, 1955.

Parascandola, John, PhD. "From MCWA to CDC: Origins of the Centers for Disease Control and Prevention." *PHS Chronicles*, November–December 1996.

Polony, Antal. "What Is a Columbarium? An Interview with Emmitt Watson." Seven Ponds, June 2, 2012. www.sevenponds.com.

Presidio. "Marine Cemetery Vista." www.presidio.gov.

————. "Pet Cemetery." www.presidio.gov.

Presidio Trust. "West of Main Parade Focused Cultural Landscape Report." June 2011.

Revised Mission Dolores Neighborhood Survey. Volume 1 of 2. Prepared for the Mission Dolores Neighborhood Association by Carey & Co. Inc. Architecture. November 11, 2009.

Rhoads, Loren. "Cemetery of the Week 30: The San Francisco Columbarium." Cemetery Travels. August 31, 2011. www.cemeterytravel.com.

Rouse, Wendy L. "'What We Didn't Understand': A History of Chinese Death Ritual in China and California." In *Chinese American Death Rituals: Respecting the Ancestors*. Edited by Sue Fawn Chung and Priscilla Wegars. Lanham, MD: AltaMira Press, 2005.

Rubenstein, Steve. "Little Girl, Rose Still in Hand, Found in Coffin Beneath SF Home." SFGate. May 24, 2016. www.sfgate.com.

Ruscin, Terry. *Mission Memoirs*. San Diego, CA: Sunbelt Publications, 1999.

Ryder, Alex. Interview with the author. 2022.

Sack, R.B., and A.K. Siddique. "Corpses and the Spread of Cholera." *Lancet*, November 14, 1998.

Salvano, Chris. "San Francisco's Lost Cemeteries & Pioneer Burial Grounds." 2017. www.chrissalvano.com.

San Francisco Planning Department. "Appendix F: Cultural Resources Supporting Information." San Francisco Housing Element 2022 update.

Sawyer, Nuala. "The Old Calvary Cemetery Grounds Are Right Under Your Feet." *Hoodline*, May 19, 2014. www.hoodline.com.

SF Genealogy. "Calvary Cemetery." www.sfgenealogy.org.

———. "Golden Gate Cemetery, AKA City Cemetery, Potter's Field." www.sfgenealogy.org.

———. "Green Oak Cemetery." www.sfgenealogy.org.

———. "Laurel Hill Cemetery." www.sfgenealogy.org.

———. "Newspaper Vitals Index, 1850, Deaths." www.sfgenealogy.org.

———. "San Francisco Population." www.sfgenealogy.org.

———. "Telegraph Hill Cemetery." www.sfgenealogy.org.

———. "Yerba Buena Island Cemetery." www.sfgenealogy.org.

SFGov. "Library Total Monthly Visitors." www.sf.gov.

Shaw, Allyson. *Ashes and Stones: A Scottish Journey in Search of Witches and Witness.* London: Sceptre, 2023.

Shelton, Tamara Venit. "Unmaking Historic Spaces: Urban Progress and the San Francisco Cemetery Debate, 1895–1937." *California History* 85, no. 3 (2008): 69–70.

Smith, Heather. "Dolores Park: A Historical Landmark?" *Mission Local*, September 16, 2011

Sullivan, Mike. *The Trees of San Francisco* (Petaluma, CA: Pomegranate Books, 2004).

Svanevik, Michael, and Shirley Burgess. *City of Souls: San Francisco's Necropolis at Colma.* State College, PA: Custom & Limited Editions, 1995.

Tsai, Shih-shan Henry. *The Chinese Experience in America.* Bloomington, IN: University Press, 1986.

U.S. Public Health Service Hospital (Marine Hospital) Archives, 1874–1996. National Park Service, U.S. Department of the Interior.

Veterans Administration. "National Cemetery Administration." www.cem.va.gov.

Virtual Museum of the City of San Francisco. "From the 1820s to the Gold Rush." Originally printed in the *San Francisco News Letter*, September 1925. www.sfmuseum.org.

We Are Water. www.wawproject.net.

Webster, Ian. "CPI Inflation Calculator." www.officialdata.org. Based on data from the U.S. Department of Labor.

Weirde, Dr. "Masons Arrive in San Francisco, Overthrow Elected Government." FoundSF. www.foundsf.org.

Whiting, Sam. "A Foundation of Bones." *San Francisco Chronicle*, May 13, 2001.

Wikipedia. "Adolph Sutro." www.wikipedia.org.

———. "Fort Miley Military Reservation." www.wikipedia.org.

Winegarner, Beth. "The Hidden, Painful History of SF's Magdalen Asylum." *Mission Local*, July 1, 2022. www.missionlocal.org.

Wright, Elizabethada A. "Rhetorical Spaces in Memorial Places: The Cemetery as a Rhetorical Memory Place/Space." *Rhetoric Society Quarterly* 35, no. 4 (2005): 51–81.

Yee, Larry. Interview with the author. 2022.

York, Katherine, and Tim Keefe. "Great Fires: June 22, 1851." Guardians of the City. www.guardiansofthecity.org.

Newspapers

Daily Alta California
San Francisco Bulletin
San Francisco Californian
San Francisco Call
San Francisco Chronicle
San Francisco Daily Evening Post
San Francisco Examiner
San Francisco Morning Call
Stockton Daily Argus

INDEX

ABOUT THE AUTHOR

Beth Winegarner is an author, journalist, essayist and pop culture critic who's contributed to the *New York Times*, the *New Yorker*, the *Guardian*, the *Washington Post*, *Wired*, *Mother Jones* and many other publications. Her books include *Sacred Sonoma*, *The Columbine Effect: How Five Teen Pastimes Got Caught in the Crossfire and Why Teens Are Taking Them Back* and *Tenacity: Heavy Metal in the Middle East and Africa*. She grew up in northern California and now lives in San Francisco.

Visit us at
www.historypress.com